Lary Bloom's CONNECTICUT NOTEBOOK

A Wry Chronicle of the Nutmeg State

INSIDERS' GUIDE®

GUILFORD, CONNECTICUT
AN IMPRINT OF THE GLOBE PEQUOT PRESS

H091123
917.46
BL

INSIDERS' GUIDE ®

Text design by Nancy Freeborn

The following stories originally were written for *Northeast*, the Sunday magazine of the *Hartford Courant*: "The Buck Shops Here," "The Final Exam," "A Visit with Beth Usher," "Semper Paratus," "Our Little Town of Bethlehem," "Scenes from Stew Leonard's," "A Yale Education," "Speechless: Sol LeWitt's Silent Night," "Miss Alyce at the Tap Room," "The Heart of Town," and "A Case of Connecticut Wining." They are reprinted with permission. All other stories in this book appeared in a slightly different form in *Connecticut* magazine.

Library of Congress Cataloging-in-Publication Data

Bloom, Lary.
  Lary Bloom's Connecticut notebook : a wry chronicle of the Nutmeg State. — 1st ed.
    p. cm.
  Collection of articles originally published in *Northeast* and *Connecticut* magazines.
  ISBN 0-7627-3894-4
  1. Connecticut—Social life and customs—Anecdotes.
2. Connecticut—Civilization—Anecdotes. 3. Connecticut—Biography—Anecdotes. 4. Hartford (Conn.)—Anecdotes. I. Title: Connecticut notebook. II. Title.
F94.6.B58 2005
974.6—dc22   2005014770

Manufactured in the United States of America
First Edition/First Printing

For Si Taubman and Suzanne M. Levine

Contents

Acknowledgments

Over the years, I benefited from the counsel of many editors whose influence is reflected in this book. These include Charles A. Monagan, editor of *Connecticut* magazine, as well as present and former *Hartford Courant* staff members Jim Farrell, Stephanie Summers, Steve Courtney, Lynn Tufts, Anne Farrow, Judith Haynes Hochberg, Dave Funkhouser, and Jan Winburn. I am grateful to Brian Toolan, editor of the *Courant*, for allowing the reprinting of several pieces that originally appeared in *Northeast* magazine.

My editors at The Globe Pequot Press, Mary Norris and Sarah Mazer, have been enthusiastic and wise partners. Mary instantly grasped the project's possibilities, and Sarah provided excellent counsel throughout the editing process. There are also those to thank who have been generous sources of encouragement, contacts, or astute feedback: Suzanne M. Levine, Jill Butler, Si Taubman, Sharon Taubman, Dale B. Salm, Marilyn Buel, Steve Metcalf, Jim Travis, Quyen Truong, Suzanne Staubach, Dale Cramer Burr, David Hays, Wally Lamb, Cindy Brown Austin, Whitelaw Wilson, Jess Maghan, Peter Walker, Jon Joslow, Nancy Dionne, and Barbara Delaney.

The Back Story

*I*n the spring of 1980, I came to Connecticut for what I thought was the first time. A colleague at the *Miami Herald* was getting married back in New England, where she had grown up. The invitation was compelling—a celebratory weekend up north in the heart of May. I still have physical evidence of that event. A photograph shows me on a dock. I am dressed in a slick gray suit and holding a cigar (a Miami habit that common sense forced me to give up). And I retain a clear mental picture of how that weekend affected me.

I think of the little white church in the village of Noank, and of the intimate reception of family and friends at Stonington harbor. But as much as the memories of this sweet wedding itself, I recall the feeling of being home. This was odd. I had grown up in northeastern Ohio, which, the last time I looked on a map, remained considerably west of Connecticut. Was it just the fragrant spring air that I had missed?

Not long thereafter, I noticed an ad that said the *Hartford Courant* was looking for an editor for a new Sunday magazine. The ad instructed applicants to write, but not to call. So I picked up the phone. I spoke to Mark Murphy, then the editor of the *Courant*, who didn't mind my impertinence and invited me for an interview.

Even so, he must have wondered about my motive. I already had a plum position as editor of a Sunday magazine with a large budget in a city brimming with news of a Cuban boat lift, racial strife, political corruption, and an otherwise impressive array of human indignities and struggles. Why come to quiet Connecticut from the world-class chaos of Miami?

At the time, I couldn't articulate the reason. And as it turned out, I didn't need to. As Murphy drove us back to Hartford from a minor-league baseball game in Bristol, he offered me the job, and I accepted without hesitation.

It was only months later, after starting the work, that it hit me. I was driving through Litchfield County to meet a writer. The countryside seemed familiar—rolling hills and dense foliage—as if I had been there before. I had a childhood image of picking apples with my father. But I hadn't, had I? It was then that I remembered how the lore of Connecticut and of my home state converged.

Growing up, I was fascinated by Ohio history. I knew not only about the obvious heroes—U. S. Grant, Thomas Edison, the Wright Brothers—but also of Moses Cleaveland, president of the Connecticut Company. This Canterbury native explored westward for hospitable farmland. When he arrived in the area that later became Ohio, he, too, felt at home—the climate, the countryside, everything but granite-hard soil. Cleaveland purchased an enormous tract from Native Americans that became Connecticut's Western Reserve. This started a migration of citizens from the Nutmeg State. Many settled in the new village named after Cleaveland (the name was eventually shortened, the story goes, because it didn't fit across the top of the newspaper). Almost two centuries later, I made the reverse migration from that area, albeit through Miami.

One of the things that had frustrated me about south Florida was that it seemed rootless. New England, by comparison, values its well-developed sense of place. Even so, I should point out that I have found here almost every species of human drama that I found in south Florida—it merely took time, patience, digging, and listening. As editor for twenty years of *Northeast*, I wrote a weekly column that took me all over the state and that introduced me to hundreds of people and places I will not forget.

A colleague once told me, "If I were a magazine editor, I would kill not to have to write a column." Editing is more than a full-time job. Most editors choose not to write, and I can see why. I was always torn between the two tasks. Staff writers and freelancers needed my attention, but sometimes I was focused on my next piece. I persisted in this schizophrenic track for all of my tenure at *Northeast* because, as much as I loved determining overall content, I also wanted to observe the community for myself and to sit at a blank screen and see if I could turn chaos into story.

My intention was always to be a storyteller. I have used the techniques of fiction—character and plot development, dialogue, and scene setting—in nonfiction writing. I taught these techniques as both an editor and an adjunct professor at Trinity College and Wesleyan University. And I put them in a book, *The Writer Within*.

In 2001, a decade after *The Writer Within* was published, I finally gave up editing to commit myself to writing full time. I left the *Courant* to work on a book and to write the lyrics to a musical rooted in Connecticut. But there was still much to discover about my adopted state. So I started a monthly column for *Connecticut* magazine.

I have selected pieces for inclusion here from both *Connecticut* and *Northeast* that address, as far as possible in one volume of modest size, what I see as the character of Connecticut and its people. I have updated or otherwise added new information to these pieces. Also, my editor at Globe Pequot, Mary Norris, had the idea of an extra dimension that would make use of my experience as a magazine editor and teacher. And so each piece is preceded by a journalistic or writing point, or something I learned along the way. This, then, is both a book of, and about, storytelling. It is limited, of course, to perceptions of my first twenty-five years in Connecticut. Unless you count, as you may aptly do, the thirty-six years that came before that.

Lary Bloom

Chester, Connecticut

Part One

LORE & ORDER

Kate's Fenwick

My intent is to develop a strong sense of place. This requires immersion in the history, lore, issues, traditions, and personalities of the community. Even so, my own perceptions may easily differ from those readers who prefer more convenient conclusions. After this piece was published, a longtime Fenwick resident objected to my historical reference to discriminatory practices in the borough. He wrote that he hadn't ever come across evidence of bigotry. This proved the publishing axiom that it is not possible to report discrimination without being accused of it. (Originally published July 2004)

In the months following the death of Katharine Hepburn, real estate rumors floated around Fenwick, the secluded borough of Old Saybrook where the actress had lived on and off since her youth. Her nine-bedroom, eight-bath house, which overlooks Long Island Sound and went up for sale for $12 million, had been examined by Dennis Rodman, basketball's most famous cross-dresser. And then by Tony Soprano himself, actor James Gandolfini.

These rumors proved false. But it is true that Robert Loggia, who appeared on several episodes of *The Sopranos*, summers in a house a short walk from Kate's. Loggia plays the same nine-hole public golf course in the borough where the actress often demonstrated her considerable athletic skills. I watched him at the second tee one day. Loggia sent the ball in the direction of the beach instead of the green. This result elicited commentary directly out of *The Sopranos* script.

Fenwick, of course, has always had star quality. Kate brought it with her, from the early days, when Hartford's Hepburns built their first summer "cottage" (as houses are called in the borough), through the devastating hurricane of 1938, and even in her later years, when the actress secluded herself at the end of a driveway off Mohegan Avenue where two similarly worded signs welcomed visitors: PRIVATE! KEEP OUT! (These signs were among the Hepburn goods later auctioned by Sotheby's.)

There were decades when Kate was much more public. She was often seen in her straw hat fastened by a large scarf (she was an early advocate of "no sun"), riding on her rusty bike or playing tennis. She was as pleasant to strangers as any other Connecticut Yankee.

Earlier encounters were recorded by Marion Grant, Kate's sister, in her book, *The Fenwick Story.* In the 1930s, when Kate was courted by Howard Hughes, neighbors were tuned in to the love affair. On a round-the-world trip by air, Hughes called his new flame regularly from exotic locales. The Hepburn family, like everyone else, had a party line. Nosy Fenwickians heard everything that went on.

The borough is small, only eighty houses or so, so it's hard to keep secrets. Still, family matters are not generally subject to public discourse.

The families that settled the place, and many that stayed for generations, were consummate Yankees who lived by unbendable rules. For one thing, they didn't wear their wealth on their frayed sleeves. The Hepburn house itself, though large and ideally situated with private access to Long Island Sound, was never fancy. Those who inspected the 8,000 square feet for possible purchase noticed its lack of modern amenities.

The rooms have a cabinlike feel. The cypress-paneled living room is large, but not extravagantly so. The kitchen is not what one might expect: no granite countertops or Sub-Zero refrigerator. It looks much like it did in 1958, when Kate played the Shakespeare festival in Stratford and when, as every summer, the place was full of family and seasonal help.

A woman who worked there as a teenager recalls that there was always a pot of congealed hot fudge sauce on the Aga gas stove. Kate and her brother Dick dipped into the pot at all times of the day and night. Lunch was a casual affair-maybe some celery and a hard-boiled egg.

During high season, July and August, there was seldom reason for the Hepburn family or any other residents to drift from the borough. The produce man brought native tomatoes, lettuce, and fruit. There was a linen man and even a traveling knife sharpener.

Fenwickians, there for a summer's privacy themselves, didn't go out of their way to say hello to the actress. The borough, however, was slowly changing from the way Kate always knew it. Summer cottages (many had not been winterized) that had been in families for generations were now being sold for millions.

An enclave that was once almost exclusively high-bred WASP was invaded by "those people from New Jersey," a code for the large Catholic families, the only ones that could fill the many-bedroom cottages. And then came the Jews. And then the Fourth of July fireworks.

Presumably, devotees of the borough's original charter have been unamused by the annual holiday noise fest. The charter gave Fenwick authorities the power "to prevent and quell riots, to prevent vice and immorality; to suppress gambling houses, houses of ill-fame, and disorderly houses; to prohibit . . . the use of fireworks, torpedoes, firecrackers, gunpowder . . . to prohibit the crying of newspapers upon the Sabbath . . . to regulate and prevent the location of pigpens . . ."

There were also demonstrations of public morality. Even after Prohibition was repealed, the Hepburn family didn't serve alcohol. How horrified the family would have been to know that just down the street, in the late 1960s and early 1970s, certain young and flowery residents were enjoying brownies made with hashish. Ah, Fenwick had clearly gone to hell.

I don't know what Kate thought of the changes. My relationship with her was not really a relationship at all. We worked on two projects, but I never met her. We had phone conversations. A typical one, on a day when I knew she was visiting her sister Marion's house:

Kate: "Hello."

Me: "Is Ellsworth there?"

Kate: "I'll get him."

Ellsworth Grant, a writer and historian and the husband of Marion (she died many years before her sister), was my go-between. I was intimidated by Kate. A lot of people were, though a friend of mine knew exactly what to say upon meeting her for the first time: "Hello, remarkable woman." To which she responded, "Hello, remarkable man."

The first time Kate and I worked together was on a memoir. I was the editor, at the time, of the newly minted *Northeast* magazine at the *Hartford Courant*. In anticipation of the first anniversary issue, I wrote to ask if she would write about her Hartford childhood. A week later, she sent me a note: "Dear Lary Bloom: If I can think of something. Katharine."

A few weeks later, her car hit a telephone pole, and she was rushed to Hartford Hospital, where her physician father had worked. While her broken leg mended, she wrote about expectations of death and about her eventual burial place, Cedar Hill Cemetery, in Hartford's south end, where the Hepburns own a large plot. The piece was full of dashes instead of periods. The way she talked. Everything was urgent.

This was the beginning of her efforts at memoir, culminating in the best-selling 1992 book *Me*. (Who else could get away with a title like that?) Kate also participated in Art for All, a public art project I was working on, recording taped interviews about her childhood for the Hartford public schools. But in my rare visits to Fenwick, I never thought to stop at her house and say hello. Such a thing just wasn't done.

Fenwick has changed, obviously. But there remains an exclusionary feel to it. If you were to head there for the Fourth of July fireworks, you would have to ask directions, as there are no signs pointing to the borough and no indication you've arrived. If you locate it, you might have to explain your business to a security guard. Such guards are hired for special occasions, and though they can't legally keep anyone off public property, they can, and do, offer a sense of courteous intimidation to casual visitors who might still be starstruck.

Kate's house eventually sold, though at a much lower price than originally listed, in the neighborhood of $7 million. Star appeal, apparently, doesn't add substantially to the value of bricks and mortar. Moreover, the kind of New York money that can pay $12 million might be obliged to spend itself in the Hamptons or Connecticut's Gold Coast, where many more Manhattan business contacts reside.

In the weeks before the sale, interest grew in the property. And why not? It's a beautiful setting, with a private beach. You can just picture Kate out there every day, going into the water, between the rocks and the lighthouse, living her life independently, frugally, and with every ounce of dash that she had. Quite a legacy for a piece of real estate.

The Buck Shops Here

Readers often ask where I get my ideas. Most are developed from whims or from a strong sense of inevitability—the subject simply calls out to me, as here. I noticed a one-paragraph newspaper article that carried the headline "Driver Hits Deer," not exactly news in Connecticut. But buried in the paragraph was this minor point: The injured buck ran from the accident scene into a nearby shop. No further details were given. It appeared up to me, then, to fill in the blanks. (Originally published July 2000)

Jerry Morgan's eyes light when he is asked to tell a story. Of course, it is what you expect of a fisherman, of someone who instructs you to call him "Cap'n" because that's what everyone calls him aboard his 17-foot guide boat and even in his retail shop.

It is something you expect of a man who wears his rich and still largely ebony hair in an abundant ponytail ("because I can") and who is not shy of delving into any subject except his age (easy enough to conclude, as he was a classmate of Johnny Egan—the basketball star who graduated from Hartford's Weaver High in 1957 and went on to college and pro fame).

Cap'n Morgan had a story to tell, for certain, and I was an eager listener who had traveled across the shoreline to hear it. Police reports from a few nights earlier indicated that his shop, Captain Morgan's Bait and Tackle, on the Boston Post Road in Madison, had been visited by an unusual intruder.

A deer circled the interior a few times and then departed the premises. The report had the young buck injured by a car. In his confusion, he sought out the Cap'n's shop for, well, what would a deer do in a bait and tackle shop?

Cap'n was on the phone when he heard a commotion at the front door. Must be some kids out there. You know how, on clear evenings, they hang around shoreline towns. So he went to investigate and was startled to see a young buck, who on his way in had deftly sidestepped the lobster pots. The Cap'n had no idea about the injury—the buck's eyes were "crisp," if a little wide. For a bait and tackle shop is confusing enough, with T-shirts that say SHUT UP AND FISH and saltwater lures that say ASSASSIN and squirmy live eels.

The Cap'n, of course, could boast of some experience with deer, but always from a distance. The area in which he makes his living is hard by Long Island Sound and the East River, where there is no shortage of sightings of deer, osprey, and herons. But he had to confess that he had never actually sold anything to a deer during the shop's three seasons.

He could see that the buck was a young thing, about three-quarters grown, and with antlers enough to stay away from. "It was my thought at the time," the Cap'n observed, "to become a part of the environment and not part of the problem." And so he watched as the deer, clearly frightened, surveyed the interior, looking past the Ocean Kayaks, past the display of LaCrosse boots and the tank of shiners toward the back, where he saw what he needed to see—daylight.

The trouble was that the daylight was showing through a glass door, and the young buck, not having a lot of experience opening glass doors or considering their purpose, decided to employ the direct route: He ran at the door as if it weren't there, aiming his antlers at the glass. But the door didn't budge.

This did not deter him. He backed up a few feet, lowered his head, and set out to overcome whatever this thing was that kept him from his natural habitat. Again, he hit the door. Again, the double-paned, safety-tempered glass didn't give, and the buck was stunned. He was not one to give up, however, and he tried again, and again, each time with the same result, except that now blood was evident and cracks in the glass began to appear. He had been injured and was certainly in a panic, which spurred him on to a different and more unpromising route to the outdoors—circling the goods over and over.

In his mind's eye, the Cap'n could see his young business trashed by a runaway buck who surely would not come out the better for it—perhaps even kill himself in the process of ruining the place. But there was no trashing going on. The buck, though clearly dazed, was the most graceful of animals in the extremely tight aisles of an enterprise consisting of a mere 600 square feet.

The Cap'n had always noticed how many inconsiderate customers brush the fancy Star Rods (costing up to $250), but the buck never touched them. Nor did he threaten the $350 stained-glass representation of Faulkner's Island by artist William Rasche; nor did he disturb the ceramic coffee mugs that say BLUEFISH,

BLACKFISH, or MAKO SHARK, or the lamps above them. The delicate fly-fishing gear and other lures that could have caught on him never became an issue because the buck, though bulky, was as deft as any animal could be in a terrified state. He couldn't help that he was dropping blood on the display cases and the floor.

Of course the panic wasn't limited to the buck. The Cap'n wanted to open the back door, but each time he tried the buck would come frighteningly near, and the Cap'n was not eager to serve as a cushion.

He managed to reach the phone and call Bruce Beebe, owner of Beebe Marine, the complex in which the shop is located. Bruce was in the back and didn't respond to the unusual phone call with, "You must be nuts. Couldn't be!" He took quick action and, with his assistant, opened the back door. The buck, however, had apparently learned his lesson back there—no longer trusting that the outdoors was the outdoors.

He tried, instead, the front door—but when he saw the traffic he got spooked. So he made more tours of the merchandise until, at last, he took a chance and went out of the door that, a few minutes earlier, he had entered, and, for an animal that had every right to complain about how he felt, ran swiftly across the field as if he had never faced misfortune.

The Cap'n went outside and saw his roadside sign moved—the work of the deer. And he saw the woman who had hit the animal with her now slightly damaged Toyota. She had been driving slowly, she said, but she hit him all the same, though there was no sign of blood near the car.

The Cap'n offered the woman a cup of coffee, which she accepted, and they talked of the incident for a while, for it was a story, a true one that, without the help of embellishments, could be told by great-grandchildren.

I asked the Cap'n how the incident had changed him. He didn't fall for the bait of a reporter, however. No self-reflection. No philosophizing. His dark brown eyes twinkled as he said, "Now I have a new motto. I tell people that the buck stops here." Yes, Cap'n. And shops here, too.

Invisible City

The best time to write about people is when they face a change or challenge—even people, as in this case, who are always eminently quotable. It is a question of stakes. If the stakes are high, the drama is inherent. (Originally published December 2002)

Down where the Hartford swells collect—the bar at the elegant brasserie, Pastis—a fellow of some influence held forth on the sad state of urban affairs. There were the usual lamentations, including the one about the city that was once America's richest descending to one of its poorest. Yes, by all means, we needed to point that out as we lifted our $9.00 glasses of imported pinot noir and thought about ordering cassoulet for dinner. And yes, didn't you think the *New York Times* was accurate in its annual page-one report on Hartford's decay?

I pointed out that although the *Times* had interviewed dozens of city leaders, in its search for depth and perspective the Newspaper of Record apparently hadn't talked to the most important person in town.

"And who might that be?" asked the fellow, thinking I might name the insurance exec who earned headlines for carrying away a

$20 million pension, or the mayor, or the chief of United Technologies. But it was none of these.

"Bill Hosley," I answered.

There were guffaws all around, as if the swells were asking, "You mean Bill Hosley, the dreamer? Bill Hosley, the man who can't stop talking about what Hartford was? That Bill Hosley?"

"The very," I said. In this life, it's more comfortable to argue the negative than to offer praise. Nevertheless, I said, Bill Hosley is everything a city visionary ought to be—eloquent, brilliant, and largely unrecognized for his accomplishments. And a recent victim of both insult and injury.

I thought of the first time I met Hosley, when he spoke about the power and possibilities of history as a tourist attraction. He referred to the relics of Hartford in very unacademic terms, as "all this neat stuff."

I remembered one day many years ago when we explored Cedar Hill, cemetery of the Hepburns and other luminaries. Hosley wasn't content to merely *show* me the enormous monument that Elizabeth Colt built in memory of Sam, her industrialist husband. He had to *climb* it. In doing so, he discovered inscriptions he'd never seen before. This fascinated him, and he climbed higher, only to lose his footing and tumble to the ground, scraping his knee against the pedestal. When he rolled up his pant leg, I could see a gaping wound. But he ignored it entirely, as if nothing had happened, and continued his case on behalf of Hartford's Colt legacy and how it ought to be a substantial part of Hartford's identity.

Back then, he had a broad vision for Coltsville, the neighborhood surrounding the gun factory. It was only years later that our two U.S. senators took up the cause of fashioning a national park out of the environs. Do you think Hosley gets any credit for the idea now? And do you think he drums up much of an audience when he talks about the "amazing riches" of Connecticut's cities, and argues that their historical sites are what we ought to invest in, not generic solutions imported from every other city in America?

Still, Hosley earned a loftier position from which to make his points than when he was curator of decorative arts at the Wadsworth Atheneum. In 1997 he became director of the Antiquarian and Landmarks Society, which tends nine historic houses around the state, including the Amasa Day House in East Haddam, where on one summer day friends of A&L gathered to celebrate its glorious collection of art and photographs. There was something else to toast on that day, too. Following a four-year, $1.3 million renovation project, the Butler-McCook House, the last private residence on Main Street in Hartford, had just reopened to the public. Hosley and his organization clearly seemed to be in for a summer in the sun.

The next morning, however, the Hartford Fire Department called Hosley at home with the terrible news. At 5:00 A.M. a Kia Sportage had barreled down Capitol Avenue to Main Street and turned everything upside down. A driver at this intersection has three choices: He can turn right and go south on Main Street. He can turn left and go north. Or he can go straight ahead through the traffic light; drive over the curb; smash into the historic, newly refurbished Butler-McCook House; rip into the south parlor; and knock down the wall that contains the valuable William Wheeler painting of Talcott Mountain, his vehicle's progress impeded only by the Everett upright piano, manufactured in Boston, circa 1900, and sturdy enough to stop an SUV before it goes through everything and ends up in the back garden, created by landscape architect Jacob Weidenmann (designer of Bushnell Park and colleague of esteemed Hartford native Frederick Law Olmsted, who designed New York's Central Park).

A few hours after the accident, nearly every friend of history in the state had heard about the damage to the textiles, carpets, ceramics, glass, upholstery, lacquer work, and other appointments. They had also seen Hosley's memo, in which he pointed out that the family who had lived in the house "stood up to the wrecking ball of urban renewal and for one hundred years fought to preserve this remarkable sanctuary to Hartford's glorious past. We urge friends of Connecticut history and material culture to extend a hand. We are determined to make it right and assure the light of Hartford's history is never extinguished on Main Street."

Vintage Hosley. Passionate. A call to action. Within days, tens of thousands of dollars had been raised to fix the damage.

I walked through the wreckage with Hosley, and he seemed uncharacteristically down. But it wasn't the condition of the house that made him so. He was confident that it would be fully restored in time and that the funds would be found. Besides, visitors would still come to the Main Street History Center, a part of the house that was undamaged.

His concern was for the city he loves. He looked around and saw money spent "on a cul-de-sac of bad ideas." If a few worthy destinations had just some of the millions the state is spending on the huge Adriaen's Landing urban renewal project, the cities of Hartford, New London, Norwich, New Haven, Waterbury, and a few others could be made much more prosperous by investment in infrastructure that's already there.

The Greater Hartford Convention and Visitor's Bureau Web site left him aghast. The home page featured only one image—a drawing of what the convention center would look like when completed. There was no link to the Mark Twain House, Bushnell Park, the Old State House, the Harriet Beecher Stowe House, any A&L property, the Wadsworth Atheneum, or anything else that makes Hartford distinctive. It would be, Hosley said, like Disney showing only hotels on its home page. "Tourists don't go to Disney World for the hotels."

Hosley knows that in cities across America there has been enormous investment in cement. In twenty years, nearly $20 billion was spent nationwide on convention centers, stadiums, arenas, and other renewal efforts. No doubt there's some value in all of that. But to him, the investment in Adriaen's Landing is seriously out of scale considering the riches already present—gems that need only to be polished.

History is a tough sell to the pinstripes. They say, "Good idea" as they really think, "Who are you kidding?" Moreover, there is the question of the poor. How will an emphasis on history feed them? Hosley answers that history is an economic generator and that there is voluminous evidence in other towns across the land to prove that. Cultural-heritage tourism is the fastest growing segment of the tourism industry.

Meanwhile, Connecticut cities such as Hartford have searched for relevance. Will Hosley and his few allies—notably the Greater Hartford Arts Council, the Connecticut Humanities Council, and a collection of notable historic sites—be able to turn the city's past into its future? "I'm surrounded by skeptics," Hosley says, "but I believe in this place."

In light of all this, was the *New York Times* report accurate? Hosley says the piece was "glib, easy, not untrue. But what will it take to spill a little ink on the things people don't know about Hartford?"

EPILOGUE

After several years as head of the Antiquarian and Landmarks Society, Bill Hosley resigned in early 2005 without public explanation.

The Perils of Prudence

Local history can be a hard sell to a general readership.
This is often because it is presented at a distance, as in
the manner of high school textbooks. I prefer to address
history, as here, with one foot in the present—giving the
reader a more obvious stake in the events and in the
consequences for the people (historical and contemporary)
at the heart of the tale. And, when ugly history is about
to repeat itself, there is the rewarding opportunity to use
the power of the pen to call public attention to the cir-
cumstances. (Originally published June 2003)

From the evidence, Governor John G. Rowland thought about the courage of Prudence Crandall on two occasions.

The first was on October 1, 1995, when he elevated Crandall, a century after her death, to the lofty status of Official State Female Hero. This put her on a par with the Official State Male Hero, Nathan Hale, who gave his life and a time-honored quote to the Revolutionary effort.

The second time the chief executive thought about Prudence Crandall, who like Hale paid dearly for her actions, was in the winter of 2002–03. He decided then that her memory was unaffordable. With the prospect of large state deficits and unions refusing to accede to his demands, the Canterbury museum bearing Crandall's name would close, along with other sites under the aegis of the Connecticut Historical Commission.

This news sent the guardians of history into a frenzy of lobbying. They'd had some practice in the recent past. For whatever his merits, Governor Rowland had never demonstrated great passion for the state's heritage.

It is true that he came around in matters of art. Assaulted by the numbers—persuasive arguments that art means big business—he lifted the category from state budgetary footnote to a chapter all its own. He became rightly proud of his effort to raise per capita spending on the arts community to the highest in the nation. But in the business of state identity and heritage, art is not all.

Historians tread lightly on this. "I have nothing against interpretive dance," Kaz Kozlowski told me on my visit in the summer of 2003 to the nearly boarded up Prudence Crandall Museum. The museum's founding director (and only remaining employee) argued that a well-rounded and refined society can't live on art alone, and that the lessons of where we came from are indispensable.

My visit to the museum was long overdue, though I'd been interested in the Prudence Crandall case from the day the museum opened to the public in 1983. I had not heard of Crandall before that, and I wasn't alone. Director Kozlowski, who grew up in Connecticut and is a well-educated historian, was also unfamiliar with the name until she was interviewed for the job. In this, we have distinguished ignorant company. Jennifer Rycenga, a native of Fairfield who studied at Yale and now teaches comparative religion and women's issues at San Jose State, had no idea of Prudence Crandall's triumphs and trials. She stumbled across them while doing other research and became so enamored of the story that she is writing a book. The tentative title is *A Life of Opposition: Prudence Crandall and Her Times.*

The Crandall story, she says, is not well known because of "the ambivalence in our society toward abolitionists." It is also true that Connecticut doesn't think of itself as a state that excludes people, though it certainly has been. Many businesses profited from slavery. And through much of the state's history, it was illegal to build a synagogue or a mosque. It also was forbidden, from 1834 to 1838, to do what Prudence Crandall did.

For those who may benefit from a brief (and entirely inadequate) accounting, I offer the following: Crandall, a much admired teacher, opened a private school for girls in Canterbury, a small community in the eastern part of the state, in 1832. She was celebrated for a time; students adored her, and so did their parents. Then she decided—after a struggle of conscience and consulting her Bible—to give twenty-year-old Sarah Harris what she so desperately wanted: a seat in her school. Harris was black, and her arrival in the classroom had dire consequences.

Andrew Judson, the town's most influential citizen, confronted Crandall. Judson was an advocate of the colonization movement, which would send blacks to live in Africa and teach Christianity there. Crandall, however, wondered whether Judson's exclusionary brand of the religion was worthy of export. When Judson raised the possibility that accepting students of color might encourage intermarriage, Crandall responded that one of Moses's wives was black.

But Crandall's staunch defense of her actions succeeded only in emptying her school of whites. She enlisted the aid of abolitionist William Lloyd Garrison of Boston to help her fill the school anew, this time entirely with "Young Ladies and Little Misses of Color."

Indeed, there were free families in New England who could pay the $100 annual tuition, and soon Crandall's school was back in business. That is, until the town rebelled in earnest. There was a successful effort to pass legislation in Hartford—the "Black Law"—which banned such a school without town consent. Crandall was hauled to court three times and spent a night in jail, though the case was never resolved. If the legal system didn't quite stop her from teaching, the mob did.

On one occasion, a fire was set at the school. On another, ninety windowpanes were smashed. It became clear to Crandall that she could not guarantee the safety of her girls. The Reverend Samuel Joseph May, a staunch supporter of the school, broke the news that there was no choice but to close it in September 1834. Later he said, "The words almost blistered my lips. My heart glowed with indignation. I felt ashamed for Canterbury, shame for Connecticut, and shame for my country."

The state eventually saw the error of its ways, when it was too late, repealing the Black Law in 1838. And in 1886, when Crandall was living out her years in Kansas, Connecticut granted her a $400 yearly pension as a way of making amends.

In the more recent past, there was irony in abundance as the state attempted to close her down again—or appeared that it would. All of this came as a big blow to Canterbury. Quite apart from its behavior more than 170 years ago, the town had embraced Prudence Crandall's legacy, proud that an important civil rights episode took place there. In fact, the town celebrated its 300th birthday in 2003 and had planned to do it at the museum. But it had to make other arrangements.

Once again, the future of the place was in Hartford hands. What value, in the end, would the governor and the legislature assign the lessons of courage? If early budget hearings were any indication, not much.

One by one, passionate defenders of state history testified, including seventh grader Trevor Rzucidlo, of Killingly, who argued that if the state can provide financial help to America's richest retailer, Wal-Mart, to build here, then it can certainly keep one of its most important historical treasures open. He concluded, "I may be just one person, but I am trying to live Prudence's story by coming here tonight. Prudence's story clearly demonstrated courage, and the power of one."

During the hearings, legislators asked, "How many people visit in a year's time?" Yes, the "how many" question. The answer: 3,500 people annually—about 7 percent of the number that see the Mark Twain House and less than 1 percent of the number that go through Mystic Seaport's gates. Jennifer Rycenga points out that historical museums, like art museums and theaters, have a great impact on tourism. But in the Crandall case, she was reluctant to rely too heavily on this point. It would have cheapened the argument.

Sometimes Kaz Kozlowski wondered if she was pushing a rock up a mountain. But children who visited the museum on school field trips always reminded her of its value. After one tour for sixth graders, Kozlowski asked if there were any questions or comments. "The cutest little girl grabbed my sleeve. She told me, 'Prudence made a decision and went against what everyone else thought. I have some friends. They want to go to the gravel bank and smoke. I would rather not, but it's been hard to say no. You know what? I'm going to remember what Prudence did.'"

EPILOGUE

The legislature eventually allocated funds to help restore the Crandall museum and to add a staff member. It opened again to the public in the summer of 2004.

Part Two

THE CONNECTICUT CHARACTER

Dance of Life

A writer always considers point of view. Through whose eyes is the story told? In this case, I expected to write about an elegant benefit ball in a gorgeous setting. Still, as always, I sought to show a human stake. When I saw a husband and wife, both breast cancer patients, dance until the band packed up, I had what I needed. In the days afterward, I asked them to recount that evening and details about their illnesses. You might think that people are private about such things, but most are flattered to be asked. (Originally published April 2003)

There was a stir at the home of John and Wanda Williams-McCormack of West Hartford. John complained about the stupid monkey suit. It had been years since he'd put on a tuxedo, and this rented one was still a problem even after three fittings. The haberdasher had gotten the sleeves wrong. Even now, the bow tie kept coming undone. John told Wanda that he'd be happier wearing sweats. But she argued that he looked devastatingly handsome.

For his part, John took note of Wanda's stunning outfit: a black St. John knit with rhinestone collar and sleeves, and matching black shoes with rainbow sparkles. The McCormacks looked like, if not a million bucks, at least a thousand bucks, which is in the neighborhood of what the evening would cost them as "Romeo and Juliet" donors to the Black & Red Ball. Ah, the things you do for charity, especially a charity, Hartford Hospital, that is so close to the bone.

It wasn't just his fancy outfit that concerned John, though. It was also the prospect of a formal affair at the Wadsworth Atheneum, where a sea of doctors would flood the place. John and Wanda have a healthy respect for physicians and have developed close relationships with, and dependence on, some. But it was one thing to show up for weekly Taxol treatments or radiation, and it was quite another to make medical small talk over "heavy" hors d'oeuvres—the food that was promised. John calculated the cost. He has long held that "the more one pays for food, the less one gets." Maybe if he stood in line enough times at the grazing tables, he would not go home hungry. Still, it could be quite a long evening, and John's endurance wasn't close to what it once had been.

In 1998 he contributed to an unusual statistic: He became one of only 1,500 men in America diagnosed with breast cancer. And three years later, he learned that the cancer had spread—the feared word, *metastasized*. Wanda was a great support, but, as it turned out, she needed support herself when doctors discovered her own malignant tumor. Indeed, the McCormacks had become a rare breast-cancer couple in Connecticut, which has one of the highest rates of such disease in the nation. At the Black & Red Ball, they would test their abilities to put it all behind them and have a good time.

As soon as they arrived at the museum, they were impressed by the cordial atmosphere. They got red roses to pin on and a chance to tour the much-acclaimed Marsden Hartley exhibit. They were overwhelmed by Hartley's bursts of color and felt like insiders when a docent told them how the show had been organized (and that it had taken seven years). The docent just happened to be the wife of a McCormack doctor. Ah, Connecticut is a small place.

The couple, as expected, saw a lot of people they know: their oncologist, their surgeon, their radiologist, and many fellow patients. They said hello to me and my wife, whom they often bumped into at the hospital's Wethersfield treatment center. (My wife, Liz, unfortunately was by then an experienced cancer patient.) John, at age fifty-six, was generally well connected anyway. He's a Hartford native who grew up in the shadow of Hartford Hospital. Like Wanda, he has been a longtime labor negotiator and an organizer of the community advisory board of the Partnership for Breast Care, the hospital's effort to provide more comprehensive treatment. (This is where we met.)

John's volunteer work was driven by what he learned, and felt, as a new patient. Like almost everyone else, he found his life overturned. Some of this was the result of the perpetual motion of the huge cancer machine: appointments, tests, blood, X-rays. The doctors were proficient at these matters, but the medical profession is not known for its adeptness at addressing the crucial psychological consequences of diagnoses: the confusion, anger, and despair over disfigurement, or those times when even friends don't recognize you on the street.

A few months earlier, at the request of his radiologist, John delivered a speech at the Learning Corridor in Hartford. He told the crowd that the doctor "suggested that since the event was a celebration, the words should be 'upbeat.' I told [him] that I was mostly of Irish descent and that celebration was something I am good at. But upbeat? Had he read *Angela's Ashes*?"

John spoke of well-meaning colleagues at work when he was first diagnosed. "One expressed sympathy for my plight and asked 'What's your prognosis?' My prognosis? I thought quickly about how best to respond, wishing I had never gone public. I replied, 'My prognosis? Why, I'm a Scorpio. What's yours?'"

He continued, "Today I have problems talking to people about my disease. I have a problem with telling people that I am a cancer survivor. The problem with being a survivor is that it seems so passive, like something that's happening to me rather than something I'm doing to prevent the alternative. Besides, being a survivor from week to week always assumes the risk that I will be voted off the island, have my torch extinguished, and be asked to leave the premises immediately."

John's oncologist, Patricia DeFusco, told me once that he uses humor as a defense, and John pleads guilty, even as he waxes about disease. "Cancer has helped me to learn from the mistakes of others—I can't live long enough to make them all myself." He also says, "No matter my despair, I must remember that this moment is always a gift. No matter my self-pity, only I can make sense out of the hand I have been dealt. No matter my pain, only I can create joy for those who are so accepting of my ways and so forgiving of my transgressions."

We bumped into John and Wanda throughout the evening at the Atheneum. I was one of several people who tried to fix his tie, which continued to come unhinged. We also saw them in several of the food lines. John had been right: The more you pay, the less you eat. But in this case, the morsels were spectacular: lamb, a squash timbale, poached salmon with pear salad. It was enough sustenance to provide energy for another of John's considerable talents.

The couple spent much of the evening dancing. The band started with a couple of slow ballads, but then the tempo picked up. The event—a "ball"—had an old-fashioned name, but rock 'n' roll is still the order of the night at modern parties. And so the dancing became furious and taxing.

After a few hours, people were leaving. It is Hartford, after all, and doctors must get their rest. The auction (which accounted for $50,000 of the $400,000 raised that evening) was finished—with winners anticipating a corporate-jet flight to anywhere within 1,000 miles, or time at vacation houses in the Berkshires and at Hilton Head—and there wasn't much to stay for, even though the band was still playing.

By 11:00 P.M. John and Wanda were exhausted, their bodies objecting to all of this joy, and they were looking for a place to sit. The Atheneum is one of America's greatest showcases for art but not much of a comfort station. Finally, they found two chairs. John took the shoes off his aching feet. He and Wanda ordered cappuccinos, and when they were done, nodded silently to each other the way couples do when it's time to go home.

But then John said, "With what we paid for these tickets, I'm going to try to get my shoes back on."

And they danced until midnight.

The Final Exam

*The most rewarding part of writing for me is to invite
readers into my religious experience—which is not a
reference to prayers or Biblical texts. When I am moved
by what I see and hear (my definition of "religious experience"), I am eager to bring the reader to the same
emotional plane through detail and narrative. This
must be done patiently, without employing billboard
language—that is, "ordeal," or "tragedy," or the ever-
popular "nightmare." (Originally published June 1996)*

**Question 1: Name three freedoms guaranteed by the Bill of
Rights.**

Lloyd George Gayle, born in Jamaica, sojourner to England, and
then a resident alien of the United States, studied that question and
ninety-nine others for the test of a lifetime.

He couldn't prepare the way he had prepared for the exams of
his youth, when he could see perfectly and read very well. Now, in
his sixties, his learning was encumbered. How does a blind man
investigate American history? He does it by recording the questions and answers, by playing the tape over and over late into the
night, and by reminding himself that he must learn all of this, that

not only is his citizenship at stake but the fate of his family as well.

He reminds himself of the young adults who are counting on him back in Jamaica: Michelle and Robert Dean and Kevin and Hyacinth and Yvette. He has received letters from his children over the years that invariably began, "Hi Dad, How keeping?" Letters that expressed concern over the plight of their father, whom they imagined helpless. Letters that nevertheless ended with vivid descriptions of deteriorating island conditions, personal deprivation, and hopes for reunion and a promising future.

Mr. Gayle reminds himself that he has not seen these children since 1976, when he left the island looking for that promising future himself. By the time he was able to return for one visit so many years later, he had lost his sight. Nor could new photographs show him Michelle's movie-star features or the way Hyacinth's daughter, little Sonia, twists her hair into braids, or the way Robert Dean wears his Jacksonville Jaguars cap—backward, of course.

Question 2: How many stripes are there on the American flag? What do they mean?

Mr. Gayle is independent and determined, but he was not alone in his quest. The other folks at Luther Manor in Middletown, a senior-citizen home, encouraged him. And so did "Miss Judy," his social worker, and "Miss Jenny," from the Visiting Nurses Association, who wrote out his checks for him and did so many other things, and particularly "Miss Sweeney," the lawyer who for three years, charging no fee, assaulted the Immigration and Naturalization Service with paperwork and telephonic pleas on behalf of her client.

Everybody wanted Mr. Gayle to succeed. There was a joy about him, a way he had of deflecting his own infirmities, which by then had become legion, and of celebrating the blessings that others enjoyed. Wouldn't it be wonderful if Mr. Gayle, frustrated so long, could finally get what he wished for?

Some of them knew his story—knew its complications and strange twists. But in the end these twists didn't matter. Like a million people before him, Mr. Gayle taking the enormous step from alien to citizen. His story was ordinary in that way. It was anything but ordinary in so many others.

Question 3: How many representatives are there in Congress?

The law of the land had become quite an object of Mr. Gayle's consciousness in the previous few years. It was not always so. Not for a one-time illegal alien. He came to the United States from Jamaica because his cousin begged him to. *Don't be foolish, mon. Leave your children. Make your fortune. Once you're rich you'll send for them, which will be very fast. Leave the beautiful land of perennial sun and perennial hardship. You know what they say about America.*

That was 1976, the bicentennial year. As the country celebrated, Mr. Gayle was, in so many ways, alienated. But he was still in his vigorous youth, or at least vigorous middle age. It is true that a doctor once told him that he had the beginnings of glaucoma, but that eye drops should help. *Don't worry.* And so he made his "fortune," a very modest one, enough to live on, working at a hotel in upstate New York. But bringing the family here was out of the question, of course, and so was going back. Illegal aliens have no rights and are in constant fear of being caught and deported, and, once deported, forever banned. And so when a general amnesty for aliens was announced, he was one of the first in line. Once finally legal, he knew that if he wanted real rights, and if he wanted to expedite the family reunion, citizenship was necessary. And he had to get professional help in order to make a way for his children.

Enter Miss Sweeney. Actually Anna Shubik Sweeney, a former environmental lawyer who took a leave from the profession to raise a family with her husband, Paul, and who, once the three children were of school age, yearned to return to work. She had known nothing about immigration law but, at the request of Connecticut Legal Services and because she was so enchanted by Mr. Gayle, took the case. There was something else, too. Anna thinks that such a case is what America is all about. She thinks of her grandfather, who risked all by emigrating from Russia to England, of the family members who came after that to the United States, and how opportunity was surely found here—her father became an eminent cancer researcher, her uncle an economics professor at Yale, her aunt a TV producer and writer. She wonders what would have happened if her grandfather had not taken that huge risk.

Question 4: In what year was the Constitution written?

In what year did things begin to go wrong for Lloyd George Gayle? You could say 1962, when he and his wife separated. You could say when, after he came to America, his relationship with a different woman in Jamaica—the mother of his children—soured. He was truly alone at that point. Or you could say it was the night in 1985 he went to bed feeling some pain in his eyes. He woke up the next morning and the lights were out, never to come back on. He remembers how his boss cried when he heard the news.

Things began to go right, although at a snail's pace, once Mr. Gayle gathered his entourage of helpers. Once Anna Sweeney began to pepper the INS—to call them up on the non-toll-free number and hang on the line for an hour, waiting to speak to someone who usually proved unhelpful. There were endless forms to fill out, to send in, to wait 90 or 120 or 180 days for replies. *Why don't the birth certificates of the children name the father? Can you show other testimony of fatherhood? A baptismal certificate? Affidavits sworn to by two or more persons who were living at the time and who have personal knowledge of the event to which they attest? Medical records or early school records? Letters between the "father" and his children showing he has sent money or otherwise watched over them?* They could do some of that. Mr. Gayle was one of the most organized people his lawyer had ever seen. He kept everything, including a letter Kevin wrote in 1989: "Dad, I know that you have it very hard on you over there, but we have it very hard, too. Sometimes we have to drink a little water and go to bed, but anyway we are still trying to live by the help of God . . ."

Question 5: What is the introduction to the Constitution?

They were questions that were hard enough in ordinary times, under ordinary circumstances, questions that many people born in this country—the automatic citizens—might have trouble answering. And with the added burdens, the test loomed large and difficult.

When Mr. Gayle was finally called to take it, he proudly announced the answers. He was not asked all of the questions, but a sampling. He was asked, for example, to name ten states, which he did with ease. He was asked what president freed the slaves. Abraham Lincoln, he responded. He was asked who Martin Luther King was. Mr. Gayle replied, "He wanted to bring peace and harmony among the races."

He answered correctly all of the questions he was asked, and he waited for the day when his citizenship would become official. Meanwhile, his lawyer pressed the INS and was pleased to report, in time, that the two boys, Robert Dean and Kevin, were cleared to come to the United States. And soon after that, that Michelle and Hyacinth could come (and Sonia, too), but that Yvette, who is married, would have to wait—her emigration would be possible only after citizenship was awarded to her father.

Question 6: What is the most important right guaranteed to American citizens?

"I bought a new suit at Regal's. I was a well-dressed man." Indeed, in the days before the citizenship ceremony in the spring of 1995, Mr. Gayle walked into the men's store on Main Street in Middletown determined to outfit himself as a gentleman. A fine brown suit. A new fedora. A pair of shoes that Miss Jenny spit shined. He couldn't see himself in the mirror, but on this, the proudest day of his life, others would see him as a man who, whatever his difficulties, stood tall.

There were people from all over the world—more than one hundred of them—that day in the federal court in Hartford. It was, according to Anna Sweeney, a sight she will never forget: "What this nation is supposed to be, accepting people from every kind of situation. You almost think the melting pot no longer works, but it does."

The judge gave a short talk. An oath was given. Certificates were awarded. Judy Baldwin, the social worker, remembers that "When Lloyd got up and walked over to get his certificate and handshake, the other people didn't know him, but they saw he was blind, and they saw his gorgeous smile, clearly so happy. And he looked smashing. The whole room burst into applause for this man. He radiated such a sense of well-being and good spirit."

When the ceremony was over, every new citizen went to the adjacent counter and registered to vote.

Question 7 (the final question): What now, my loves?

His children arrived on the night of May 23, 1996, after a long flight from Kingston to New York and a limo ride from JFK. Anna Sweeney and I weren't there to see the hugging and the crying and the praising of the Lord. But the next morning we drove to Pearl Street in Middletown, where the determined Lloyd George Gayle, in anticipation of his arriving family, had purchased a home for $68,000 after arranging private financing from the seller. It is a lovely two-story that is pleasant and accommodating; he trusted that it would make a perfect starting point for his family of immigrants.

The walls inside were bare—this is the house of a blind man—except for the relief of the Last Supper that the occupant crafted at the Day Club for Seniors in Middletown.

The family sat around the living room that morning—four children (Yvette had not yet been able to come)—and talked about themselves and each other at my urging. They were funny, charming, shy, eloquent. Michelle, age twenty, told me she wanted to become a cosmetologist. Robert Dean, twenty-five, said that he had aspirations in mechanical drawing and architecture, but that he might continue to do what he did in Jamaica—stand-up comedy. Michelle said, "You never know when he's serious." She seemed reticent. Part of what she was feeling became clear when she said that she already missed her mother. Kevin, twenty-two, wanted to go into computers and thought he would get that chance. "Jamaica is beautiful," he said, "but there is more opportunity here." The children remarked that their father looked well and that if he had stayed in Jamaica, the sun and the hard labor would have long ago killed him; men perish too early there. Hyacinth, twenty-six, said, "I'm so glad to be with him. I prayed it all the days of my life."

That morning, we talked of the promise of America, of icons such as Patrick Ewing, of getting jobs and education, and of getting ahead. We talked of the wonderful Russell Library just down the street that would introduce them to so much they needed to know, and about how to get Social Security cards (which they knew about already). Their father, in a matter of hours, had briefed them on the way America runs.

Anna Sweeney and I thought the same things (after comparing notes later): about how bright these children are, and how they seem to know that success won't come easily, and how they surely know that what their father did for them is something they can never repay—except by doing their best in this country.

When the curiosity and conversation ebbed after a couple of hours, Kevin—sensitive and sincere Kevin, wearing his Cape Cod T-shirt—gazed at his blind father sitting in his chair, and at his siblings sitting around the room. He turned to his father's lawyer and said, softly, "God bless you, Miss Sweeney."

A Visit with Beth Usher

One of the most memorable pieces I published as North-east's *editor was Nancy Metcalf's account of a seven-year-old girl's profound medical trauma—and the removal of half her brain. As the child grew up, I developed a friendship with her, and a little more than a decade after her surgery, I offered this update of her condition and outlook. I tried here to weave the past and present, so that those who hadn't read Nancy's original piece could still get a sense of what it contained. (Originally published January 1998)*

Beth Usher answered the door and invited me in.

"How are you?" I asked.

"Awesome," she replied.

Then she amended her answer to something akin to semi-awesome. She hadn't gone to classes at the high school that day because of an ear infection. "Nothing serious," but enough to keep her home.

I hadn't seen Beth for six years, since I met her one night on the University of Connecticut campus when she was twelve. That was the year she had been in the newspaper again—her letter had convinced Fred Rogers, the star of the popular children's television show *Mister Rogers' Neighborhood*, to come to Storrs to deliver the UConn commencement speech.

Now Beth was grown, or at least older, a wise eighteen, although not much taller than she was a few years before. She walks slowly, favoring her left side. She also favors that side in her conversations. She asked me to sit on the couch and then took a seat to the right of me, which, I understood, allowed her to see me comfortably, with full peripheral vision.

She told me about her part-time job as a teacher's aide for an after-school kindergarten program at Dorothy Goodwin Elementary School, not far from her house in Storrs. "I play with the kids—make sure they don't get into trouble." I wanted to know if she liked the job. She said, "I know now never to have kids of my own." She paused, then said, "Just kidding."

She said the kids sometimes act up, and they think they can get away with it because she's not as old as the teacher. "So I put the dunce cap on their heads." Again a pause. "Just kidding."

She didn't kid about the sweet day several months before when the kids planned a surprise birthday party for her. They hid under the table, in the dark. She thought that something was wrong and that the school had closed for the day. But then the kids all started to giggle and said, "Happy Birthday, Beth." That was June 29, the day Mister Rogers called; he always called Beth on her birthday.

A few days before the visit, Beth asked me if I knew about the upcoming *Dateline* show on television. She explained that she and her parents would watch. It would make sense for me to watch, too, because the show was to focus directly on the issue that darkly colored Beth's early life, and that still provides perplexing shades of gray.

Not that Beth or her parents were eager to see the program. *Dateline* would follow a child, in this case a thirteen-year-old girl, through the very same procedure at Johns Hopkins Hospital in Baltimore that Beth had undergone there when she was seven. This patient, like Beth, suffered from Rasmussen's encephalitis, a very rare condition found in young children in which inflammation in the brain causes seizures and, if untreated, proliferates and totally debilitates its victim. The only reasonable treatment is what may seem like an unreasonable one—the timely removal of the entire diseased half of the patient's brain. When Beth went into surgery, it had been undertaken only sixty-eight times in medical history.

The Ushers watched *Dateline* together. In observing the terrors and frustration of the particular family that was featured, Kathy recalled all of her own emotions during the time her daughter suffered one seizure after another, without their having any idea why. Kathy remembered being out of control, calling doctors, demanding that the hospital admit Beth. She remembered facing the news that her child would require the most radical surgery of all, and that Beth's precious brain cells were dying, and that, if this risky procedure were not undertaken, she would be fit only for an institution. Kathy remembered how little patience she'd had for anyone. When friends would complain about their nails, "Internally I would say, 'Oh, my God, they have no clue.'"

The television program showed it all, up close, and the Ushers recalled precisely what Beth went through at Johns Hopkins. It took surgeons several hours to remove the left hemisphere, the part of the brain traditionally thought to control language. The surgeons also split the thick band of nerve fibers, the corpus callosum, cutting off communication between the various lobes and preventing the spread of seizures. It was, of course, a traumatic operation—so much so that four patients have died during or soon after surgery. Beth's response was a thirty-two-day coma.

Kathy Usher remembered all this and got up from the floor, in tears. Brian squirmed in his seat. Beth was stunned. "I couldn't believe that I went through all of that." She doesn't recall her own operation, except through the documentation of family photographs and stories.

People who come into contact with Beth for the first time and observe the clearest residual effects of her surgery wonder about her limp and her weak right hand. So they ask. Beth tells them, "I was injured in Vietnam." Or, on other days, she might say, "My scientific experiment went totally wrong." Or, "I went bungee jumping without a cord."

She was, her mother remembers, always a child who had great humor. And now humor serves Beth well, as her weapon and as her shield. The day of my visit I heard it many times, particularly when Beth and I were alone in the hours before her parents came home from work.

"What should I ask your dad?" I said to her.

"Does Beth get an allowance?" she replied.

But there were serious questions, too. It is a crucial time in Beth's life. She is on the cusp of her independence. After graduating from E. O. Smith, she plans to go to college. But she feels the very strong pull of home and is of the opinion that her parents won't want her far away. "They'll be worried," she said.

"Should they be?" I asked.

"No."

Then she said, in typical Beth fashion, that perhaps she could do something to make them change their opinion about wanting her nearby. "I need to be more evil. I can change, honest I can."

Not likely.

For here is what happened not long before when Kathy Usher received flowers at work (she is the head of UConn's scholarship office): She thought, how nice of Brian to send her a bouquet. (He works as assistant admissions director and was, for several years, an assistant football coach.) Her coworkers were impressed that Kathy's husband would be so thoughtful. But the flowers were not from Brian. They were from Beth. Everybody who had a teenager at home, or ever knew a teenager, or remembered their own teen years, commented on how unusual and special it was for a mother and daughter to be so close. Beth, in a moment of candor, said, "Give most of the credit [for her recovery] to my mom and dad. They never gave up."

Their closeness is one of the rare benefits of what Beth and her family endured. Yet all these years later, with Beth still limited physically, she has forged other relationships that point to the good that can come from awful turns of events.

She is a pen pal to children who face the disease she had. She is highly thought of by her classmates at E. O. Smith for her positive attitude, and for always having a good word to say.

One of the teachers, Ursula Laak (now retired), told me, "Beth's thoughtfulness has many times almost made me cry. When a day was tough and she realized other students were hard [for me] to manage, she would leave a little note. 'Hang in there,' it would say . . ."

The enthusiasm for Beth's attitude and work habits extends up the scholastic ladder. During my visit, I saw a letter from the superintendent's office. Beth was one of two students who would be honored at an upcoming award ceremony.

"Why were you chosen?" I asked Beth.

"Maybe it's for being the friendliest senior. Or maybe I cut class, or punched a freshman, or swore at the teacher."

We are caught, as journalists, in an emotional and professional trap. We seize upon an inspirational story—the story of Beth Usher is surely that—and yet we tell ourselves, and our readers, that we are dedicated to truth. What is the truth here? There is truth in the notion that Beth has made a courageous return from a terrible illness, and has done so with the help of a loving family (including her brother, Brian Usher Jr., who is studying at UConn's Avery Point branch). It is true that she is doing well at E. O. Smith, well enough to be regularly listed on the honor roll among students of her level (she still requires some special education classes).

But what of the real, lingering issues in the life of Beth, and of the Usher family? Can we put a smiling face on those? It's complicated, to say the least. There is some difference of opinion in the house about how far Beth can stray from home when she goes to college. Beth is confident she'll do nicely wherever she is. There is, perhaps, too, a difference between Beth's dreams and the realities that might be commonly predicted for her. She desperately wants to become a teacher. Will her physical limitations disqualify her? The things that many teenagers take for granted—a driver's license, for example—may be beyond her reach.

And there is this lingering matter: the trouble she has with short-term memory, another souvenir, apparently, of the radical surgery. It may have something to do with the limitations of a single brain hemisphere trying to accommodate all learning and experience. Because of the condition, she must study harder than "ordinary" students. She must write everything down. She must rely on the commitment of her parents and of special teachers who understand both Beth's limitations and her gifts.

And there is the matter of dealing every day with the looks and assumptions that can come from anywhere, from any source. Her former teacher, Ursula Laak, says, "She knows what prejudice is. People look at her and may make a comment. [As a result] she feels very deeply for others. She tries to protect them."

Beth has her own way to express the phenomenon, in poetry, the medium where honesty comes most naturally. She writes:

> Don't stare at me,
> Stare into me.
> See the real me.
> Feel my loneliness and my hurt.
> I am me but
> could be you.

And still there is something unquantifiable about Beth Usher, something her mother, Kathy, knows inherently—a quality that can't ever be measured by IQ tests or ordinary yardsticks. The Usher family was reminded of it a few years ago after a dispiriting visit to a doctor who revealed that Beth had to undergo a major operation on her back to correct severe scoliosis, another consequence of her old condition.

Kathy remembers, "We were driving home. We were so shocked we couldn't even speak. Beth was sitting in the backseat. She said, 'Come on, guys. It's not like I have to have more brain surgery.'"

And so the somber mood changed. The family stopped at an A. C. Petersen store and, Kathy remembers, "We went bananas and started throwing ice cream at each other."

Also from the works of Beth Usher: When she was twelve, she wrote a booklet for children who were about to enter the hospital. It was called *The Sun Can Come Out Again, or: How I Got Rid of Something Bad!* She dedicated the booklet to Ben Carson and John M. Freeman, the doctors at Johns Hopkins who saved her life, and she listed fifty rules for surviving in the hospital, including:

> *Make your brother or sister wait on you . . . It's the only*
> *time they will.*
> *Make sure doctors talk to you. As an adult.*
> *Pretend you're asleep when people you don't like visit you.*

The last reminded us, oddly, of Mister Rogers, whose visits solicited no pretending on Beth's part. During Beth's profound illness as a small girl, Kathy wrote Mister Rogers to tell him the magical effect he had on her daughter. The only time of day she could be certain Beth wouldn't suffer seizures was during his afternoon show. Kathy asked if Mister Rogers would be so kind as to write or to call. As it turned out, he didn't do either.

After Beth's brain surgery, when doctors feared her coma might have profound consequences, he traveled from Pittsburgh (his headquarters) to Baltimore to visit his new little friend in the hospital. Fred Rogers sat at Beth's bed that day, took out his puppets, including King Friday and Princess Tuesday, and performed a private show for her. He spoke to her as if she were listening.

A few days later, Beth emerged from the coma with these words: "Dad, my nose itches me."

Years later, she wrote to ask Mister Rogers to speak at UConn's commencement, explaining that her mom was head of the committee. "It would be an awesome idea if you spoke." He accepted. Then he asked Beth for advice. What should he say in his remarks? Beth wrote back with suggestions. "I told Mister Rogers to tell students to do good deeds for other people so those people could help other people."

She, of course, went to the ceremonies and remembers well his opening words: "It's a lovely day in your neighborhood." He then read the letter that she sent to him.

A few days after my visit to the Usher house, I called. Beth talked about some of the things she'd meant to tell me, about her swimming (she's very good at it) and how rabid a fan she is of the UConn women's basketball team (she once went on the team bus to a game in Providence, and she goes to all home games with friends and relatives).

I asked Kathy about the letter Beth had received from the superintendent of schools. Kathy told me about the ceremony the family attended and the special award given to Beth. It was for being the most improved student at the high school. "She had to go up there on the stage, stand there while he talked about her. He talked about how she had the ability to look on the bright side and to cheer people up."

There have been times, Kathy said, when she has felt a sense of profound loss—about how Beth will never take Irish dancing and never experience the feeling of getting on the stage to perform.

On the other hand, Kathy feels blessed that she still has her child—her child who is about to go off on her own. But, perhaps, not too far.

EPILOGUE

In 2005 Beth turned twenty-five. She is still living at home, and she still volunteers every afternoon at the Dorothy Goodwin Elementary School. She never enrolled in college but did join AmeriCorps for two years. In this capacity, she taught "the love of words and reading" to four- and five-year-olds in Windham. Beth told me that her greatest satisfaction during this time was a breakthrough with an autistic child who started to communicate with her.

Communicating with children remains an important goal to her, and she hopes that the booklet she wrote as a twelve-year-old will have wide circulation.

Her more recent writing includes an appreciation of Mister Rogers, which Beth wrote when he died in 2003. In the piece, commissioned by *Northeast* magazine, she wrote, "The universe was crying today, birds stopped singing, children stopped laughing . . ." And she went on to recall his important role in her recovery, giving him much credit for the restoration of her sunny outlook and for setting the kind of example that "can make the world a better place."

Semper Paratus

One of the duties of the writer is to break down stereo-types—to sweep away assumption and generalization by focusing on the particular, on human detail. All the members of a military band may dress alike, wear short hair, and play flawlessly. But that's where the similarities end. Each story is individual and unique but, once collected, contributes to a full historical and contemporary portrait of an ensemble that is universal and yet like no other. (Originally published October 1996)

They are but four of the forty-five musicians who make up the U.S. Coast Guard Band, one of Connecticut's, and America's, cultural treasures. They are men and women in uniform who study not war but harmony. They came together from little towns in Florida and Wisconsin and Ohio and from one very big city in Russia because it was their destiny. They came together to demonstrate the power of music to eliminate boundaries and to lift the soul.

THE SINGER

She was educated and talented, and she was underemployed despite being just a dissertation short of a musical doctorate at the

University of Cincinnati. Then she noticed a classified ad in *Musician's Union*, the trade paper for performers. Wanted: a band singer.

For Tracy Thomas, a military band seemed an unlikely employer. But holding down several low-paying jobs at once and waiting in vain for opera companies to call can convince a soprano to try anything. She sent off a tape that showed that her scholarly credentials didn't inhibit her from appreciating popular standards or from emulating Cleo Laine, one of her favorite jazz singers.

Despite stiff competition, Tracy soon found herself as a finalist in an unfamiliar city called New London. At the band headquarters of the U.S. Coast Guard Academy, she performed for people who seemed anything but military in their demeanor and their enthusiasm for her artistry.

They loved her polished voice, her stage presence, and her interpretation of popular songs and were intrigued by her resume, which listed operatic work. The band was looking for such versatility. With forty-five members, it is the smallest of all of the country's professional military bands, and so its musicians must be nimble in a variety of musical styles—everything from Count Basie to Dmitri Shostakovich.

The singing job that Tracy applied for was a new position. Through its seven-decade history, the band had collaborated with many notable vocalists—Roberta Flack, William Warfield, and Michael Bolton among them—but never had an official, full-time singer. The time had come. The repertoire could become more varied, and besides, the addition would echo the influence of John Philip Sousa, who advised the band at its beginning and who always featured a singer in his own bands.

At the audition Tracy belted out jazz arrangements and then

sang a Mozart aria. Soon after, she was offered the same job as the other triumphant auditioners for the band: Musician First Class (E-6), with an annual salary of about $25,000, uniforms, and trips around the country and the world. She also had the chance to sing the music of her choice and the obligation otherwise to perform only "collateral duties," such as working to secure sheet music and helping with administration. For these musicians, all highly trained, there are no sea rescues or drug investigations.

And yet, during the time she was given to make her decision, Tracy's friends back at school tried to talk her out of it. In fact, they laughed at her. Her professors, however, did not laugh. Do it, they said.

So she did. Her mother was thrilled. "I have life insurance. I have benefits," Tracy said. "As for my friends, they're sitting in Cincinnati, doing clerical jobs for temp agencies."

The Percussionist

The band that Tracy Thomas joined had long ago welcomed its first woman, although Connie Coghlan might have wondered about the definition of *welcome*. The percussionist was aboard the band bus back in 1973, when the language used by the fellows was ungentle—guaranteed to offend tender ears from Fort Atkinson, Wisconsin, just as the heavy haze from cigarette smoke annoyed any uninitiated nose. Otherwise, Connie found herself instantly among friends, enjoying a camaraderie and security that few musicians know.

Her arrival was a memorable moment for one of the band's most loyal fans. Elizabeth Neilan, a New London teacher who never missed a local concert over several decades, always sat in the front row and always delighted in the program, whether it was heavy with military marches or Dixieland or the serious concert music that the band has introduced to its audiences over the years. After each performance Mrs. Neilan came on stage to speak to Connie and to other band members.

The audience for this band has always been loyal; the concerts (always free) at Leamy Hall are usually played to capacity crowds. However, 1973 belonged to another era in American military history. In the last years of the Vietnam War, Connie marched in the band's outside row during parades, close to the crowds. She wondered if someone out there might take out his objection to the war on a woman beating the drums.

In the years since, however, the most overwhelming feeling by far has been joyous—one of reassurance and of family. Connie works with dear friends in a close-knit group that history shows has come closer than any musician could anticipate. People have come to New London for a hitch and stayed a lifetime. Some got hitched in the process. Connie points to the day when the two-person tuba section married the two-person bassoon section.

And she points to the sad days, too, when this great family of musicians was in danger of being a broken family.

THE CONDUCTOR

He is a gentle man, the sort of fellow you might not think of as a commander in the military. His duties are not only to conduct and direct the band, to write arrangements, and to compose, but also to demonstrate by example the professionalism of the Coast Guard. He does this through an assemblage that is thought of as one of the best—perhaps the best—of the service bands.

Lewis J. Buckley was not necessarily commander material when he was a kid growing up in a little town in Florida, and then in Miami. His trumpet fascination led to an excellent education at the Eastman School of Music, where in a competition he was chosen to be trumpet soloist with the Rochester Philharmonic.

When the Coast Guard Band needed a trumpeter, he applied, thinking that an old school chum was in New London, so how bad could it be? It turned out that his chum was in the Navy Band, but Lew Buckley stayed in New London. In 1975, only six years after his arrival, he became the youngest conductor of a major military band since the days of Sousa. Buckley was twenty-seven.

There are memorable moments to recall in his nearly three decades on the podium. The band has played for presidential inaugurations and presidential funerals. It has played the Kennedy Center and Carnegie Hall. It played in England on the fiftieth anniversary of the D-Day invasion; afterward, a former British soldier, in tears, explained to Buckley that it was the U.S. Coast Guard, during the invasion of Normandy, that rescued him at sea.

These concerts might not have occurred had the Coast Guard brass been able to follow through, in 1982, on planned economy measures. It wanted to cut the size of the band in half and move it to Washington, D.C. Buckley fought to keep the band intact and to allow its members, long ensconced in the community, to stay in Connecticut. But at the time he was only a musical lieutenant and, in the hierarchy of the Coast Guard, played the part of first-chair pipsqueak. He was obliged to make out a list of those who would stay and those who would go. He remembers band members who didn't have families who volunteered to give up their jobs. He remembers that during those days, "The sky was a different color.

The trees were a different color. That's how depressed I was. Other than when my father died, it was the worst thing I've gone through."

The change was to take effect April 1, 1982. A few days before, at a rehearsal, Buckley told the band, "I'm sorry, there's nothing more I can do." He will never forget their response: applause for the conductor.

He remembers, too, the support of loyal fans within the Coast Guard itself (Rear Adm. Arnold Danielsen was one who stood up to authority) and of old friends such as Mrs. Neilan, the school-teacher, and Dick Coburn (also a teacher), who has been making the drive from Athol, Massachusetts, to New London for more than thirty years to attend concerts.

Connie Coghlan, the drummer, remembers that on March 30, 1982, only hours before the big cutback, Channel 8 news reported that all of the passionate lobbying had helped persuade authorities to reconsider. "The Coast Guard Band has been saved!" It was a transforming moment, one that made possible many transforming moments since.

In 1989 the U.S. Coast Guard Band became the first American military band to play in what was then the Soviet Union. Although it was the time of *glasnost* and *perestroika*, the musicians had no idea what to expect in the way of a reception.

They certainly didn't expect thousands of Leningrad citizens to stand for so long during their concert and to be so appreciative as they played, among other selections, Leonard Bernstein's "Overture to Candide," Duke Ellington's "Sophisticated Lady," W. C. Handy's "St. Louis Blues March," and, of course, "The Stars and Stripes Forever." They surely didn't expect what happened during the encore.

Also performing that day was a Leningrad military band. One of its members, a trumpeter, took it upon himself to join in as the U.S. Coast Guard Band played "When the Saints Go Marching In." He traded eight-bar solos with the American soloist. The crowd loved it. The musicians loved it. For a few minutes East and West, and all political boundaries, blurred. When the encore was over, Buckley and the soloist from the Soviet band embraced, and he remembers thinking, "Everything I have done in music since I opened the trumpet case in the third grade has led to this moment."

THE PIANIST

When the Coast Guard Band played in Leningrad, Ian Frenkel was nineteen years old and studying piano at the Gorki Institute. Ian (pronounced Yahn) was a musical prodigy and came from a musical family. He lived for many years with his grandparents in Moscow. His grandfather was a jazz violinist who loved Cole Porter and played in the style of Stephane Grappelli, but because of the Cold War, he was frozen out of the larger jazz world.

Ian's own parents, who were divorced, had long since left the Moscow neighborhood. His mother had gone to Italy and sent for him a few weeks each summer. And back in 1979, his father had explained that he had a chance to go to America, alone. Leonid Brezhnev had made it possible for many of the country's Jews to emigrate, and, facing limited opportunity at home as a scientist, the elder Frenkel had no choice but to leave. He would write soon, he said, to tell Ian of his whereabouts, but it was a promise he couldn't keep. Those who left the country were terrified to write home for fear that the families they left behind would become outcasts.

It wasn't until ten years later that the father was able to send for his son. The two met at JFK airport. His father expected a child, not a man wearing a beard who had grown to be 6 feet, 8 inches tall. Ian had expected a younger man with a beard, not the clean-shaven, graying man who called him son. Nevertheless, the two recognized each other, and Ian began his new life.

He soon became a jazz pianist in Manhattan, playing clubs as a sideman but seldom sitting in the audience as a fan. He couldn't afford the cover charge. Until the day he saw the ad in *Musician's Union*.

THE MUSIC, FIRSTHAND

In the summer of 1996, the band played at the fiftieth anniversary of the Hill-Stead Museum in Farmington. The pops concert began as usual, with "Semper Paratus" (meaning "always ready"), the stirring Coast Guard official march. The band went on to play Sousa, Copland, Borodin, and, featuring singer Tracy Thomas, songs made famous by Judy Garland. It also played its usual interlude of Dixieland jazz, which featured a nice riff on "Back Home Again in Indiana" by Ian Frenkel, the new pianist from back home in Moscow.

As the band played, men and women in the audience smiled and tapped their toes. A little girl who could not have been but two years old, wearing a purple dress and holding a pink balloon, danced to the music as if she had heard it all her life—which at that point was almost true.

Anyone, two years old to one hundred or more, can take advantage of the uplifting programs of this band at one of its many free concerts. But it's too late to sit next to Mrs. Neilan, the New

London teacher. The longtime fan of the Coast Guard Band and tireless champion of the arts suffered from Alzheimer's disease for many years. Her condition deteriorated to the point where she had to live in a nursing home. On Memorial Day weekend in 1996, she died at age eighty-nine.

At the wake someone told her son, Lawrence, about the lovely reference to his mother that had just been made at Leamy Hall. During its annual Memorial Day concert, the band members dedicated a piece called "Praeludium," by Armas Järnefelt, to the person who had supported them for so long: Elizabeth Neilan, the woman missing from the first row.

Part Three

A SENSE OF PLACES

Our Little Town of Bethlehem

Sometimes ideas are so obvious that nobody sees them.
For many years as an editor at Northeast, *I tried to*
interest photographers in a Christmas photo-essay on the
many communities in Connecticut that have Biblical
names (Bethlehem, Goshen, Canaan, Bethel, etc.).
Finally, one holiday season I set out on my own to paint
a word picture of one of them. (Originally published
December 1997)

THE SHOP

In this lovely community in the Litchfield hills, enterprises thrive
that don't automatically remind a visitor of Christmas. For example, there is the unisex beauty salon Hair It Is. There is Abe's East
Street Deli, where the hot chocolate earns high ratings. For more
sophisticated drinking there's the village wine shop, which, in the
ancient spirit of the community, is called a wine shoppe. The
Towne Apothecary displays a large array of Hanukkah cards. But
there is also, not surprisingly, a perpetual sense of Yuletide. The
name of the town is enough to do it. And then, of course, there is
the impressive emporium called, appropriately, the Christmas
Shop in Bethlehem.

It has been here since the late 1970s, when Joan Smith opened it before the nationwide boom in year-round Christmas peddling. Maybe you remember Joan Smith. Maybe the woman dressed in green (handsome green blazer and pleated green skirt) on the day I visited was your English or history teacher at some point long ago. She used to make her living that way in the days before she had a vision for this place, back before she and her husband, Sheldon, moved to the big farmhouse on this property that was large enough for their six children. But even if you didn't have her for a teacher, you'd sense there's something to be learned here.

I asked for a tour of the displays of merchandise that she loves, and Joan mentioned the impact of the reunification of Germany. One of the great beneficiaries of the old Communist system was the proliferation of irresistible handmade symbols of Christmas. The small ornaments, the figurines, the nutcrackers that emerged from the Erzgebirge area of the old Democratic Republic were made by craftspeople whose work was subsidized by the government. Much of it is no longer available, Joan reported, although she did point to the variety that remained.

This is not to say that the shift from communism to a free market didn't have its benefits. She showed me exquisite gift sets of handblown glass ornaments from Poland, including likenesses of Rhett Butler and Scarlett O'Hara. Here was Sherlock Holmes with Watson. Here was Betty Boop and Snoopy and an array of antique cars. All made possible, presumably, by the uprising Lech Walesa started down at the Gdansk shipyard.

Surely things have changed from the time Joan opened the shop. In those days a typical customer came to a store like this to find calico and straw. Nativity scenes were a curiosity and not a mania that would draw those interested in, say, the Fontanini collections, hand painted in Italy. The full villages, too, have become collectibles. Joan showed me a few in the old milk cooler outbuilding, which was the site of her first store. You can see there an entire New England town (one of the buildings is that of John Pierce Boat Works), the Dickens village (with the Old Curiosity Shop), even the North Pole (with a place called Giggleswich Mutton and Lamb). In another area of the place is a display of beautiful caroler dolls made by the Byers family in Pennsylvania.

I asked Joan when the shop closes on Christmas Eve. She said about 3:00 P.M., so the "wonderful people who work for me can have a little Christmas Eve of their own."

The Post Office

Every town has a post office. But there is something unique about the home of zip code 06751. Back in 1938, Earl Skidmore Johnson, who was postmaster here for forty-one years, sent a card to the U.S. postmaster in Washington, D.C. He decorated the front with a rubber stamp, showing a Christmas tree and the words, "Merry Christmas from the little town of Bethlehem."

A tradition was begun, and every year since then, a new stamp, or "cachet," has been added to the collection. It is a collection known all over the world, for each holiday season the post office receives boxes of Christmas cards from far-flung people who would like their cards decorated with an image from America's "Christmas Town."

But you needn't mail yours off to enjoy the service. You can come here to the lobby to stamp your own cards with any of the dozens of cachets designed since 1938, or you can watch small children do the same as they experiment with shapes and sizes.

One of the children who came here during holiday seasons long ago grew up to be the present postmaster. Joan Manzi is a woman of tradition, and she is eager to hold on to this one. To a degree, she laments the way Christmas has changed from a holiday where children were overjoyed to receive just one present, and probably a handmade present at that. In her time, she provided a few of that variety to her three children and ten grandchildren (the girls swooned, reportedly, over the red jumpers, and the boys appreciated the red vests). Now it's a computerized world and, no avoiding it, a greedier world.

Vera Rosa can verify that. She is the post office employee who has been Santa Claus since 1995, taking over the role played by Barbara O'Neill for more than two decades. Vera, who grew up in Bethlehem, moved off to California, and was drawn back here by the town's sanity and charm, answers the letters to the North Pole. She replies to all of the year's requests, including the one she has just read from a boy named Joey, which is surely detailed if not entirely organized:

> *1. I want a go cart, with gas.*
> *2. And a trampoline.*
> *Dear Santa, I want a little snowmobile.*
> *I want a Nintendo, Number 64.*
> *The last thing I want is a diamond.*

What's a Santa to do? She'll do what she did the year before and what Barbara, as Santa, did before her—call the parents to find out what's really possible and make a hint of it in her reply. And while's doing it, she'll drop the name of the family cat or dog, a sign of warmth and familiarity.

But sometimes the requests are hard to respond to, as in the case of a little girl named Katy. The postmaster and Santa know her, the way they know just about every little girl in this town of fewer than 3,500 citizens. Santa looks at Katy's long list and says, "Poor darling, she probably won't get anything. They have no money." For even in a town that has an increasing number of New York weekenders, there are citizens who sometimes can't make ends meet, even at Christmastime. And so you would wonder about this letter:

Dear Santa,

I've been good all year. Can I please have a Magnavox stereo, Winnie the Pooh doll travel set, Fingernail Fun, Mini-mushroom three-piece set, Nickelodeon, Talkblaster Phone, Conquest Smart Station, a children's printer . . .

And, as if that wouldn't be hard enough to answer, there's Katy's P.S.: "Santa, are you really real? All of my friends say that you aren't."

Vera and I talked of the proper way to respond to the child's particular wishes (in which Santa would write that maybe Katy won't get everything she wants but she'll get something nice), and the matter of Santa's very existence. What we have here is a modern-day counterpart to little Virginia O'Hanlon, who wrote to the *New York Sun* more than a century ago with the same question, worded almost the same way. The query prompted a front-page editorial by Francis P. Church, who answered, "Yes, Virginia, there is a Santa Claus." In this case Vera Rosa, who knows that little Katy's friends are probably even more cynical than Virginia's were, would write something like, "The spirit of Santa is real."

The Pizza Parlor

The building that used to be the post office back in Earl Skidmore Johnson's day is now Theo's Pizza, although Theo doesn't run it anymore.

I learned this from a nice couple in a corner booth having lunch. Joseph Ardwin and his wife, Christine, are in their nineties. They drive up every Friday from Heritage Village in Southbury. "We like the congeniality here, and the food is excellent," Joseph told me. I see the congeniality firsthand. The Ardwins were thrilled to be waited on by a young woman they hadn't seen for months, and she was just as pleased to see them. There was a fair amount of hooting and hollering and hugging.

I flagged down the waitress, who told me that she is the daughter of the owners and that she lives in Greece. I asked her name. "It's kinda hard to spell," she said, pouring my decaf, "but if you have time . . ." And so Chris Mangafakis went on to tell me the circumstances of her life and her parents' lives. She lives in Rhodes, which is where her uncle Theo now lives, and is a physical therapist. She was back here, where she worked for several years, because her mother, Daisy, whose real name is Desphina, was about to enter the hospital. Chris talked of the special nature of the town. "It's not really a town, but a big family." Particularly in this place.

An off-duty state cop came in and hugged Daisy and Chris. Stefano, who is Daisy's husband and Chris's dad, carried a bouquet of flowers to the table occupied by the old couple, the Ardwins. "For you," he told Christine. "Why?" she asked. "Because you're beautiful," he replied, "and in my country, we say flowers go to the flowers." Chris joined in the celebration, wished Christine a happy birthday, and said, "The flowers are really for putting up with us."

For a few minutes, Daisy visited me while I finished my baklava (delicious and not too sweet). I asked about the hours of the place, and she told me it's seven days a week, about twelve hours a day. "What kind of life do you have?" I asked. "No life," she said, but here, which is what they love. She loves the customers, who bring her homegrown tomatoes and cucumbers. And who, no doubt, would bring her other things, too, after they found out about her scheduled neck and back surgery in Hartford. Daisy was confident she'd return to what amounts to her home before the doctor thought it was wise.

The Creche

Writing about the character of a town is a presumptuous undertaking, particularly by a casual visitor. There are any number of places where time and space do not allow exploration, including the beautiful Bellamy-Ferriday House and the old Catholic church (across from the post office), where Joan Manzi's children were married and which lost its steeple. Then there are matters about the community and its everyday life that would escape those of us who do not traverse Litchfield County all that often. I'm told of the continual struggles to pass school budgets and of the traditional political infighting. In a sense, this little town is like any other, with cliques and power bases and elements that can make for unsettling headlines. But there is no denying either that there is a special feeling here. The people knew it—natives and New Yorkers alike—on the night when almost everybody showed up at a benefit at Memorial Hall to raise money for a boy who needed an $18,000 wheelchair (the goal was exceeded by $7,000). You can see it for yourself every December when 20,000 people show up for the annual Christmas Town Festival.

And you can see it in the guest book down at the Abbey of Regina Laudis, where people from all over the nation have come to view the creche maintained by the Benedictine sisters.

For here, on the town's outskirts, is the very heart of little Bethlehem, a place to repair to, to be silent and reflective. It is a place to view the interpretive work of Neapolitan artists of the eighteenth century who interpreted the story of Christmas in the way that would mean the most to them. You can inspect the remarkable physicality of Naples, including its crumbling stucco buildings on small hillsides. You can identify with the crowds of lords, ladies, beggars, servants, and workmen who are inspecting the Mother and the Child with a mix of curiosity, skepticism, and great reverence. You can stand there alone and consider these words from Isaiah: "Then you shall be radiant at what you see, and your heart shall throb and overflow." And in the little town of Bethlehem, you can almost touch the real meaning of Christmas.

The Hammer

When I undertook the reporting on this piece, I was in the throes of depression following the death, after twelve years of illness, of my wife, Liz, in the spring of 2003. I had trouble focusing. But I knew that if I got involved in a story and then went out to the site and talked to people there, that the usual would happen—I would become emotionally involved in the circumstance, and the piece would write itself. One other thing—the interview with Walter Lowell at the end was something of a gift. Liz always said, "What goes around comes around," and in this demonstration of it, Lowell gave me details of his own torment that he gave no other reporter. (Originally published November 2003)

The walk from Applegate Farm to another world requires all of five minutes. When Jean Bouchard, her husband, Pete, and I took this brief journey from their produce barn, our conversation turned from a new species of apple, Autumn Sunshine, to a new species of local development.

Right next door, beyond the yellow excavators and the sign that warns BLIND PEDESTRIAN AREA, is all that remains of Canton's rolling and lovely golf course: a flat expanse of dirt.

"It looks like Iraq," Jean said. We stood on the edge of what Pete used to refer to as Cardiac Hill, on the old sixth hole. The Bouchards have been among many in town who told me of the value of the old course, but I had my own memories.

This is where many years ago, Canton's longtime pro, Walter Lowell, taught me his strange philosophy of the game—that golfing should be fun. "Life has too many aggravations. Do you need another one?" It was where he revealed to countless students the secret of the proper, relaxed grip: "Don't kill the canary."

For forty-eight years, the man with the sweet swing and generous smile was a fixture at the Canton Public Golf Course, which was owned by the Lowell family. Those days are gone now, and there are only a few physical hints of the course that remain: a touch of greenery at the back end, and the red barn that served as a storage shed.

This space was to become the "Shoppes at Farmington Valley," including a Kohl's department store, a Shaw's Supermarket, a chain bookstore, and a variety of boutiques—all of them filling the last available open space along Route 44, Canton's main drag and primary commercial district.

Jean Bouchard, who has lived in Canton for more than three decades, told me that coming home from Avon on Route 44 one day, just after the trees on the course had been cut down, she didn't recognize where she was and for a moment was lost. "I know we've got to do something about taxes in this town, but this makes me cry."

And so we have, in a community of about 8,900 souls, the story of much of Connecticut: change from rural to something else. Canton's situation is not so different from that of Norfolk, a few towns farther west on 44, which was featured in the *New*

Yorker because of a dispute over turning a treasured piece of land into a luxury golf course and housing development that many luminaries—including, supposedly, Condoleezza Rice—wanted to buy into.

Canton's controversy is different is some ways. It is less star-studded, and it is about a golf course disappearing rather than popping up. But the root issues are the same. Residents ask about the character of the town and the cost of "progress." A local survey reveals that the small-town atmosphere is what residents value most, followed by its natural setting. On the other hand, the survey also shows great frustration with real estate taxes and the need to bring in commerce to ease that burden.

Canton native Henry J. Bahre, who at age seventy-four has a long-term view of the town's struggles, argues that the new commercial development "will turn out fine and serve its purpose," and will even turn out handsome, no matter what it looks like now.

Jean and Pete Bouchard invited Bahre to their house to chat with me about how Canton has been transformed over the years. Bahre, who owns a real estate company, took a seat in the family room, removed his cap, and waved off the controversy. "This town, despite its disagreements, is very cohesive." He foresees hundreds of jobs created by the development and a huge boost for the tax base.

It was Bahre who more than three decades ago created the first commercial district on Route 44—Canton Village, which was instantly embraced by town officials because back then there was a great need for shopping convenience. Canton had always been remote. There was an era when some workers in Hartford's insurance mills took a commuter train on Monday morning and didn't return home until Friday night, having stayed all week in apartments in the city. In the last couple of decades, suburban sprawl arrived, and Canton proved a more affordable alternative to posh Avon and Simsbury.

In its days as a factory town—the factory being the Collins Company in the Collinsville section—about a third of Canton's residents were employed in making axes and machetes. Houses were built for workers. A few years ago, these little places were selling for $10,000. Now, as Bahre points out, they go for twenty times that. Collinsville has had something of a rebirth as an area for artists and specialty-shop owners. "Today," he says, "Collinsville cherishes its reputation as a place with history."

But the problem, says Bahre, is that towns always must pay the price of progress, and most residents of Canton—particularly those young professionals who escaped to the countryside—have no idea that if you want to move forward, you have to give something up.

Bahre, whose great-grandfather wound up in Canton as a tailor after emigrating from Germany, grew up 3 miles from the ax factory. He remembers the trains that brought in raw steel, and the way the steel was melted to be forged into tools. "A huge drop hammer came down—you could hear it at 7:00 A.M. all over town. And every thirty to sixty seconds after that, except for a break at noon. Not a person in Collinsville would live with that today."

Bahre likens the development of the Shoppes at Farmington Valley to the Collins Company's great noise. "It just has to be done," he says. You can't, he argues, have the home owners alone carry the tax burden. With new four-bedroom houses springing up everywhere (there are about 500 available housing lots townwide, including about three dozen that Bahre owns in the prestigious Hoffmann Farms area), the schools are overburdened.

And, finally, Bahre says about the new commercial property: Everyone in town will shop there.

I thought about my old golf teacher Walter Lowell and the fall-out from all of this. He hadn't really been forthcoming in press accounts, and I wondered if he would be so with me. When I called, I could tell that it remained a sensitive subject for him. Even so, he seemed pleased to be able to tell his story to someone he trusted.

Back in the late 1980s, when I took lessons from Walter, he told me that his two brothers were pressuring him to sell and take the profits from developers. As a golf course, the land did not provide a luxurious living. But Walter persisted. He could hear his late mother, Ruth Evelyn Wheeler Lowell, saying, "Hold on to it."

It was only when he approached retirement age that Walter agreed it was time. The Lowells offered to sell the course to the town. The reaction to that was largely indifference, except for the hostility.

One man stood up at a meeting and said, "Why does the town have to bail out the Lowell brothers if they can't manage their own money?" Another suggested that the Lowells, if they were really interested in Canton, would donate their land to the town.

Walter replied, "The day you give your retirement and all of your inheritance to the town, then I'll think about it." To hear such criticism must have been particularly hard for a man who always let the town's kids play for free on Saturday evening, and who kept the greens fees among the lowest in the state.

Over the years there were plans for a sports complex there, and then an assisted-living facility, both of which would complement the natural beauty of the grounds. But the hard economic reality was that there was more money to be made by commercial developers, and the Lowells eventually wound up selling the property to one of them for $4.77 million (of course the sum had to be split among the brothers).

Walter misses the place. And he gets teary on occasion, as when a local dentist sent him a poem he'd written about playing the course, or when former students tell him about the years of enjoyment they've had playing the game. Or when he thinks of his older brother, Jim, who died in early 2003.

The new hammers are pounding now. And when the Shoppes of Farmington Valley open, there will be many residents who won't blink an eye or have any notion that right there, in the detergent aisle, a person could hit a solid 6-iron, watch as the ball landed softly on the green, and walk happily into the morning sun.

EPILOGUE

The Shoppes of Farmington Valley officially opened in the spring of 2005, though many stores had opened earlier. In the first tax year of operation, the Shoppes' bill was $880,000, which, in a time of increased spending on schools, helped keep the mill rate steady. The Bouchards go to the new development occasionally. Jean likes the children's department at Kohl's, where she buys clothes for the youngest of her five grandkids, and she and Pete sometimes have their morning coffee and bagels at Panera Bread Company. The Bouchards also attended a town meeting at which there was a discussion about a possible new tenant for the Lowells' old (and now refurbished) storage barn—Golfer's Warehouse.

The UConn Quiz

I got the idea for this piece from the amount of space that newspapers devote to the sports teams at our largest state university. In preparing it, I knew I'd have sympathetic sources—professors and others at the university who were eager to show that UConn is something more than an arena and stadium. In the actual doing, I chose reader participation, which is always popular with readers—but I did it with a twist. (Originally published September 2003)

As you know—as you must certainly know—a new football stadium called Rentschler Field opened in East Hartford in late summer 2003. There on autumn Saturdays, fans cheer the UConn Huskies and the state's nearly $100 million investment in what might be called Athletic Studies.

You have had no trouble finding ample press coverage of the games at the new stadium. My point here is simply that the UConn football team—and the men's and women's basketball teams, which have become obsessions in our state—are connected to an actual university. This university has classrooms, professors, and students, and it is becoming much more academically competitive than it ever was before, though you'd hardly know it from most media coverage.

It may be properly argued that the euphoria over the 1995 women's basketball team was the real impetus for UConn 2000, the legislature's billion-dollar infrastructure investment. And who can measure the worth of the multiple national titles brought home by the women's and men's teams? Even so, for a century or more before those championship seasons, the Storrs campus was far more than a place for gifted athletes and coaches.

With that in mind, I have prepared the following ten-question quiz. It is limited, as it must be. There is much more to the campus than represented here. And I haven't referred specifically to the branches, the graduate schools, the law school, or the medical school. The answers, as you will see, are obvious. It's the questions that you probably would never guess. They will test your knowledge of what campus insiders argue is a world-class university versus what many Connecticut folks, though they can't be blamed for this, simply consider to be the world headquarters of Geno Auriemma and Jim Calhoun.

1. Few people use the words *Storrs* and *Berkeley* in the same breath. One of them is this UConn English professor (since 1974). She has written and edited a number of acclaimed books on the Beat generation, and her friends included Allen Ginsberg, Gary Snyder, Ken Kesey, and Jack Kerouac, on whom she is the supreme literary authority. Of the working habits of the writer of *On the Road*, she once said: "Most people are, at heart, good people, but fairly conservative. They really like to think there's a tried-and-true way of writing, and you sit and write

thirteen revisions. And when they hear that he's bragging that he's written it in one draft, they kind of get their hackles up." This distinguished biographer's name is:

   A. Rebecca Lobo
   B. Sue Bird
   C. Ann Charters

2. At 10:30 A.M. on June 10, 1999, a calf was born to a Holstein heifer at UConn's Kellogg Dairy Center. Here's how it was done, according to the head of UConn's Transgenic Animal Facility: "We took a simple ear skin biopsy (a one-minute procedure) and used the cells for cloning. The embryo was cultured for seven days in the lab and then transferred to a surrogate mother. A few months later . . . our first clone, Amy, was born, weighing ninety-four pounds." The scientist in charge of the first successful cloned calf experiment is:

   A. Kara Wolters
   B. Charlie Villanueva
   C. Xianzhong (Jerry) Yang

3. This campus institution is archiving the papers of Nelson Mandela and the African National Congress during apartheid's last days. It is also a center that documents the struggle for human rights everywhere. At its heart is a collection of Holocaust materials (accessible to everyone) collected by someone who once served as a lawyer at the Nuremberg trials, later became a U.S. senator, and is the parent of another U.S. senator. This campus and world resource is called:

A. The Ben Gordon Research Center

B. The Diana Taurasi Research Center

C. The Thomas J. Dodd Research Center

4. This popular professor in the physics department explores black holes, time travel, quantum cosmology, and Einstein's theories. He is:

A. Randy Edsall

B. Richard "Rip" Hamilton

C. Ron Mallett

5. In a state brimming with wonderful museums, one gem is the William Benton in Storrs. The world-class architect engaged to design its new building is:

A. Khalid El-Amin

B. Swin Cash

C. Frank O. Gehry

6. He is the founder of a faculty rock band called Off Yer Rockers. Much of his teaching in political science is on revolutionaries, such as Marxists and the Basques in Spain, and on broad social movements. (Well, he does have a PhD from Berkeley.) This author of the much praised *A Rebellious People* is:

A. Emeka Okafor

B. Nadav Henefeld

C. Cyrus Ernesto (Ernie) Zirakzadeh

7. Like many distinguished authors, this professor of geology had a signing for his book *Stone by Stone* at the UConn Co-Op bookstore, one of the best independents in the state. Suzanne Staubach, manager of the general books division, says, "Taking a walk with him is like taking a walk through eons of history. He sees a stone, a pebble, a cut in the road, and immediately places it in its historical context. You end up becoming as excited as he is." His name is:

    A. Donyell Marshall
    B. Doron Scheffer
    C. Robert (Thor) Thorson

8. He is internationally known for his work on geospatial data. As head of the Map and Geographic Information Center at the Homer Babbidge Library, he digitizes historical maps. The library's huge collection, available at www.lib.uconn.edu, houses old maps of every Connecticut town. He is:

    A. Ray Allen
    B. Denham Brown
    C. Patrick McGlamery

9. Okay, let's throw in a little sports here. Ichiro Suzuki and Hideki Matsui are among the famous baseball players from Japan. But it so happens that the history of players of Japanese descent in America can be traced to Storrs. In 1943 UConn was the first school in the state (Yale refused, as did others) to enroll students who had been interred in detention camps. Two of

these students were members of the UConn baseball team the following spring. For such historical references we turn to the founding director of the Asian-American Cultural Center. Her name is:

   A. Jen Rizzotti
   B. Svetlana Abrosimova
   C. Angela Rola

10. Bart Roccoberton Jr., an associate professor in UConn's Department of Dramatic Arts, has taken on a university tradition begun by the person who made the art of puppetry a scholarly phenomenon. The founder once said, "We are puppeteers, and our greatest gift—to create life—enables us to radiate this life-shaping force into the world outside and to bring peace and joy and greater understanding to all mankind." The author of this quotation is:

   A. Ann Strother
   B. Barbara Turner
   C. Frank Ballard

Answers: If you answered C to every question, you've made the dean's list, and you'll be introduced at halftime at the next football game at Rentschler Field.

Scenes from Stew Leonard's

Balance is usually defined as presenting both sides of a story fairly. Like a lot of rules, it is untenable. For one thing, there are always more than two sides. And almost never in real life are all sides equally weighted. It is up to the writer to create the proper tone—to be able to say something unique and useful even as he remains fair to the parties involved. In this instance, a piece about a legendary Connecticut business where a felony was committed, newspaper headlines had given one impression, but I was intent on a more intimate view. I got it by literally hanging in the aisles. "Ordinary" people are quotable and believable after you spend more than five minutes with them and they stop giving cursory responses. (Originally published September 1996)

KITTY'S CORNER

Kitty never knows where she will be stationed in the World's Largest Dairy Store, which has been featured in *Ripley's Believe It Or Not!* Yesterday she worked the lettuce. Today she works more visibly. She takes her post in the aisles, singing the praises of a product called Boca Burgers as she fries them, cuts them up, and, in her lovely Irish brogue, urges shoppers to try this "very healthy" alternative to hamburgers. "It's made of soy," she says. "That's S-O-Y." And, "It's so fine with a slice of onion."

A woman approaches and murmurs, "Boca Burgers, huh?" She takes a toothpick and a sample, but before eating tells Kitty, "My mother-in-law is from Boca [Boca Raton, Florida]. She's been telling me about them. They'll try anything down there." The woman chews and then nods, as if to say it is perhaps possible to replicate hamburger by mixing soy with purified water, natural vegetable flavor, spice, dehydrated onion, cheddar cheese, garlic, and carrageen.

Kitty knows perfectly well the magic of carrageen, an edible seaweed. When she was a child in Ireland, when she was still called Catherine Boone by her parents and growing up in County Roscommon, her mother fed her carrageen when she had a sore throat.

On this day at Stew Leonard's, Kitty is golden throated ("I got a gift for the gab"), getting almost everyone to sample the goods and quite a few to pop a package in their carts. Kitty's routine is part of the store's culture. (Today most customers could not get through the door on the way in without sampling the fresh pineapple.)

Kitty revels in the store's fine reputation as a place of the freshest goods and exuberant customer service. I ask her if she is bothered by The Troubles, in this case referring not to Northern Ireland but to the difficulties of the store's founder. She says, "No. And I hope your article is nothing but positive."

I tell Kitty, a fervent guardian of Stew Leonard Sr.'s reputation, that the bulk of it will be positive. I tell her that many newspaper readers have been introduced only to the legal matters, which I am obliged to refer to, given that a major white-collar crime was indeed committed here.

Most readers haven't drawn their impressions of this place first-hand; there are much closer places to find sustenance. On the other hand, there is the matter of nourishing the soul and having a high old time doing it.

A first-time shopper is likely to notice immediately features that long ago made this the Disneyland of food stores. At the first stop, the bakery, shoppers and whatever kids may be in the carts marvel at the little wooden baker performing his acrobatic routine. They can't help but inspect the bottling plant that produces ten million quarts of milk each year. They hear the "Farm Fresh Five"—milk cartons and butter sticks and baby chickens—sing about the merits of dairy products and, just around the aisle, watch the routine of "Cindy Celery and Larry Lettuce," the mechanical vegetables, as they musically point out the virtues of greens. Along the way, kids play at the wishing well or press the button to hear the moo of the toy cow, to whom they compare the real barnyard animals outside.

There is the amusement park that caters strictly to older tastes: the wall of fame, with personal messages from celebrity shoppers, including Henry Kissinger, Martha Stewart, Rodney Dangerfield, Dolly Parton, Pat Riley ("Great popcorn"), Billy Ray Cyrus, Barbara Bush, Ted Koppel, Jack Klugman, Steve Allen, Michael Bolton, and Joanne Woodward ("The groceries were delicious"). On the other wall: Photographs from around the world—from France, Russia, Indonesia, Turkey, Israel, Wales, etc.—feature regular, if less famous, customers holding Stew Leonard bags; for these poses they earned $3.00 gift certificates.

Shoppers walk through the maze of aisles, all one way, past the store's coffee bean roaster, past the meat market that specializes in filet mignon from Dodge City, past the stand that helps sell 7.8 million ears of Connecticut corn every year. They invariably notice the store's legendary guidelines: "Rule 1. The customer is always right. Rule 2. If the customer is ever wrong, re-read Rule 1."

Regular customers know all this. A man and woman from Scarsdale, having just arrived at Kitty's station, talk about how for twenty years they've come from Westchester County every week. The man says, "I used to drive a limo. I picked up [Stew Leonard Sr.] in New Jersey. He was with Frank Perdue and a few lawyers in the backseat. I kept my ears closed because I didn't want to hear too much." As for the store, he says, "It was always a joy to come here. I remember how Stew Sr. would greet us by name." He says his favorite food in the store is the Key lime pie. "I could eat it for breakfast."

Kitty says, "Strawberry rhubarb, that's my favorite," as she points to her stomach. "You can tell by lookin' at me."

I ask the Scarsdale woman for their names. "I'd better not tell you," she says. "My husband works with the cops."

At Chef George's

Chef George Llorens remembers the Paris market of his childhood and thinks of it when he comes in each day and catches a whiff of the fresh produce in this store. Chef George (which is what his name tag says) owned Dameon's, then Le Paradis—a French restaurant not far away in Westport—when Stew Leonard

Sr. was a customer, long before Leonard began to eat prison food exclusively. When Le Paradis burned down in 1992, Leonard offered George a chance to improve the section of the store that featured prepared dishes.

On this day he pays Leonard, the one-time door-to-door dairyman, sincere compliments. George says, "He is an excellent husband, a wonderful father, an excellent boss to work for. He leaves me carte blanche." I ask him if he has seen Stew Leonard Sr. lately. George says that he has, and that "he looks wonderful." Chef George also says that what happened to his boss was unfair. I don't argue; it would seem insensitive on George's turf to point out even the obvious: that skimming $17 million from the profits and not paying taxes on it, which is what Stew Leonard Sr. admitted to doing over a ten-year period, deserves the sentence he got—fifty-two months in federal prison, plus three years of supervised probation. (He also was ordered to pay $15 million in back taxes, penalties, and interest; a $650,000 fine; and $97,000 to cover the cost of his incarceration.)

So I change the subject, and I ask him about his celebrity customers. He says Paul Newman is very careful about what he eats. "He loves fresh vegetables, broiled salmon, Dover sole, littleneck clams—the smaller the better. He always says, 'Choose me the smallest ones.'"

On this day Chef George's shelves feature fat-free gazpacho, carrot and ginger soup, and pasta dishes. There is also black bean dip, a container of which George holds as he points out its virtues. A shopper approaches and says, "It's very good, but it doesn't last. It ferments." George, no doubt alarmed to hear such opinion in the company of a writer, smiles his Parisian smile and says, "It all depends on if you put it in the trunk of the car on the way home." George urges her to try the "lovely chicken soup." The woman says, "I'm sure it's good, but I'm Jewish. I always make my own chicken soup."

When Chef George tends to other duties, I talk privately to the customer, whose name is Susan Geller. She tells me that she, too, has shopped here for many years—since long before the owner's 1993 conviction—and goes out of her way on the ride from Easton, where she lives, to Stamford, where she teaches. Like others, she tells me about the quality of the store and about the customer service. She tells me that she once bought about $85 worth of groceries and gave the clerk a $100 bill. She received $4.00 and change in return. Later, she discovered that she had been shortchanged, returned to the register, and in a few minutes had her money.

It's a place that always seemed to be honest, which is the trouble. Because the founder turned out to be profoundly dishonest. And when it was discovered he had hidden the millions from the IRS and everyone else, the picture changed, and suspicion reigned. Then to add to the difficulties, the state Department of Consumer Protection reported evidence of widespread short-weighting. It ultimately led to a settlement in which the store, while admitting no wrongdoing, paid $13,900 to the state.

Longtime customers such as Ms. Geller faced a decision. Stew Leonard fell from a great height; he had been honored by President Reagan and showcased as one of America's finest retailers by Tom Peters, author of *In Search of Excellence;* he had been praised by thousands of customers, celebrity and otherwise.

For a time, Geller decided that she wouldn't come here anymore, but then she thought better of it. "We put Stew Leonard on a pedestal, and it turned out he was just as vulnerable as the next person. We all have [these tendencies] in us. He's paying for it. He got caught. There are plenty of other people who don't pay."

KITTY'S CORNER REVISITED

"What happened while I was gone?" I ask Kitty.

She says, "A few of my boyfriends came by to say hello to me."

She advises that I get to know all sides of the store and some of the employees. Referring to the many countries represented in the workforce, she says, "Of course, lots of the help here don't speak English."

A woman walks by and says, "I speak English. And Hungarian, too."

Kitty laughs, sees me writing it down in my notebook, and admonishes me, "Remember, nothing but positive."

"Mostly positive, Kitty," I reply.

ALONE WITH STEW JR.

A few days later, we are up in the second-floor offices, Stew Leonard Jr. and I, talking about his father. He wants, obviously, to stress the positive. He remembers the walks he took with his dad early in the morning. He speaks with reverence of a self-taught man who studied for two years at the University of Connecticut's agricultural school but who had to quit and come to work at the old dairy when his own father died. He talks about how his dad started simply here, then built additions as needed, twenty-six of them, and a second store in Danbury that opened in 1991. He remembers all the accolades. (The *Ripley's* reference is for selling 2.9 million quarts of orange juice in a year, a world record.)

Stew Jr. remembers the year the Norwalk store opened, when he was a shy fifteen-year-old who proudly stocked shelves. He remembers his dad telling him that stocking wasn't enough, that little Stew should go out in the aisles, get to know the customers, become their friend. Stew Jr. objected. "I'm just a kid," he thought. It took twenty customers passing by for him to get up the nerve to say hello to just one.

"I always reminisce," he says. And he adds that the last few years have been tough. "And still are tough. Before all this happened, all the great articles came out—a big story in *New York* magazine, among them. Now, reporters are calling your home, trying to dig stuff up. And you feel a little ashamed when you're driving your kids to school."

There is no real defense here. Stew Jr.'s father admitted that he took the money and, after he was caught, admitted that it was wrong and went off to prison.

Not surprisingly, Stew Jr. defends his father at the same time he understands that what his father did was indefensible. In a close family, there is need for forgiveness, for unconditional love.

Stew Jr. remembers so many important moments in his own life when his father supported him—from the time when he and his Ithaca College pals went out on an extended toot, which resulted in the wreck of Stew Jr.'s new car, to the much more serious day when the twenty-one-month-old son of Stew Jr. and Kim Leonard drowned in a swimming pool. He remembers all this, and on this day, he thinks about what he will do two days hence.

The drive to the Federal Correctional Institute at Schuylkill in Pennsylvania is roughly three hours. And on the next visit, he anticipates, "My mother will sit there with her hands on her lap, and my father and I will talk from 8:00 in the morning to 3:00 in the afternoon about the stores, about how we painted all the vans with black and white cow spots on them, and how we're doing with my mother's creations"—Mrs. Leonard's Marinara Sauce and Mrs. Leonard's Balsamic Vinaigrette.

They'll talk, perhaps, about plans for a new store in Orange and possibly offer thoughts on whether to build someday in Newington. Stew Jr. will compliment his dad on his weight loss (from 194 to 174 pounds) and the shape he is in for a sixty-six-year-old veteran of a triple bypass. And they'll dream a little about next spring, when the prison term is over and Stew Sr. comes home. And perhaps back, on a modified basis, to the store that he still loves.

Stew Jr. argues that customers can separate his father's crime from the store itself—that they trust the store. As for the charges of short-weighting, he says that, despite the settlement with the state, there was no wrongdoing. He says that the store is known for its bargain pricing and for giving away more free samples than any other store.

Record revenues of close to $100 million a year tend to support the view that customers have made their peace with the place. On the other hand, he asks what I've learned from customers. How do they really feel? I say that my survey is skewed, unscientific. I talked only to people in the aisles. They are all, by definition, loyal customers. They are convinced that they are getting a good deal here. But, no doubt, something subtle has changed.

Stew Jr. does not argue. And our conversation ends pleasantly. We walk out into the parking lot to say goodbye. We pass a group of Japanese visitors who are taking a seminar at "Stew U.," where thousands of businesspeople have come over the years to learn the particulars of customer service, Leonard-style. On the way to my car, I also pass an employee of Stew Leonard's dressed as a cow. The cow waves goodbye.

EPILOGUE

Stew Leonard Sr. was released from prison in 1997. Stew Leonard Jr. is now the chief executive of the company. In 2004, for the fourth year in a row, *Fortune* magazine named it one of the hundred best places to work in the United States.

A Yale Education

Interviewing famous people is sometimes off-putting. When, for example, I called the actor Edward Norton, a Yale drama grad, while reporting for a piece about his former theatrical agent, he admonished me for straying from the anticipated line of questioning. On two occasions at R. J. Julia Booksellers in Madison, I found radio jock Don Imus intimidating, though I knew that most of his hostility is just shtick. At times such as those, I wished that I had opened a shoe store instead of pursuing journalism. But other celebrities have been much more accommodating, and they remind me that no, this isn't such a difficult business after all. When I tracked down many former Yale undergrads for this piece, they were all eager to help promote their alma mater. (Originally published March 1998)

Perhaps you saw it—the issue of *Vanity Fair* that bypassed New Haven and Cambridge on the way to Providence. The magazine pronounced that it isn't Yale or Harvard that deserves the title of the hottest Ivy League school. Brown proved the campus of choice for the children of Diana Ross, Carly Simon, Calvin Klein, Steve

Forbes, Marlon Brando, and (we're talking step-daughter here, of course) Ringo Starr. "A-list New Yorkers" and "beautiful young things," as *Vanity Fair* described them.

What's poor old Yale to do? It doesn't make a habit of revealing student celebs. The PR department wasn't even permitted to confirm the enrollment in New Haven of the Crown Princess of Sweden, the eldest of King Carl XVI Gustaf's three children. Still, it eagerly provided for me an undergrad A-list of its own going back decades or longer.

Sinclair Lewis, William F. Buckley, Jodie Foster, Tom Wolfe, a handful of Bushes, Paul Mellon, Thornton Wilder, Garry Trudeau, and Benjamin Spock all had dinner at the Commons, looked around at that dark and well-appointed cavern, and wondered what they had gotten themselves into. They had gotten themselves into the school in which Noah Webster learned the nuances of words, in which Henry Luce found plenty of conservative fellowship, and in which Cole Porter wrote the classic lyrics of an Eli fight song: "Bulldog, bulldog, bow wow wow . . ."

The list, of course, goes on. I perused it in the hopes of finding a few grads who in the wake of *Vanity Fair's* declaration would explain to me, and to everyone else who didn't have the privilege, the meaning of a Yale education. I hoped to learn the lasting effects of four years amid the stacks of Sterling Memorial Library (where the phone booths look like confessionals) or among the rare manuscripts at the Beinecke (where you can read chapter and verse, if you know the German, of an actual Gutenberg Bible) or in classrooms, transfixed by renowned professors. Where to begin? Well, not in Kansas.

CALVIN No. 1

The boy who wanted to become a writer was expected to attend a university close to home—in Kansas or Missouri. Calvin Trillin remembers that "applying to Harvard was kind of like climbing up to the top step of the county courthouse and declaring yourself a sissy." It was his father's idea that he go to Yale, though "I'd never heard of Dostoyevsky or Greenwich." Young Trillin had heard of Shakespeare. "Sort of."

Yale was a recommendation for which the elder Trillin took some heat. "Many friends told him it would be a terrible mistake—that I should be going to school with people I'd be in business with." Calvin's father was a grocer who later owned a restaurant. A fancy Ivy League education would be of no use in such enterprises. But the father was determined. He saved rebate money—one of the bread companies offered incentives for putting its product on the front shelves. And so in the fall of 1953, there was enough ($1,600) to cover the first year's tuition and room and board.

Trillin showed up in New Haven in awe. "People looked like they had costumes on—tweedy sports coats, patches on the elbows. I'd never seen things like that." Of course, he saw men's costumes because the faculty was certainly a male bastion, and so was the student body. In those days, Yale was not a study in diversity.

It was, however, a place that made an enormous impression. He enrolled in courses taught by "the Spellbinders," superstar faculty members such as Vincent Scully (architecture), Cecil Driver (political science), and Richard Sewall (literature). Like others who talked of their Yale years, Trillin recalled how New Haven changed him profoundly. "It deflected my life toward the East and away from home, and it opened a lot of possibilities that wouldn't have occurred to me."

This extended to his being chosen eventually as a trustee of the Yale Corporation. "In my day [as a student], the Yale Corporation was made up of sixteen Protestant gentlemen—literally Protestant and literally gentlemen—plus the president of Yale, another Protestant gentleman. The idea of riffraff, like writers, getting in, well . . ."

Trillin, like so many other grads, passed the Yale tradition down. In the years since the place went coed, both of his daughters enrolled and graduated.

WHAT A CARD

Sandra Boynton, who is known largely for creating greeting cards that, among other things, cleverly acknowledge birthdays, complained, "Do you expect someone in her forties to remember something so long ago?"

But she does remember. She was headed to Princeton because her dad went there. Even so, "I looked at Yale. I loved the physical being of the place, the Gothic architecture, the courtyards, so many architectural details."

She remembers her professors, particularly the Shakespeare expert Maynard Mack. "He's everything you'd want a scholar and a human being to be: brilliant, passionate, wise, insightful, humble, absolutely illuminating."

To Boynton, Yale presented a sense of infinite possibilities—which led to the kind of creative thinking that made it possible to sell eighty million greeting cards a year, a body of work that has done much for the image of hippos and other generally ignored species. It's just that kind of animal-instinctive mind that could think up—as she did—a way to employ an old Yale connection (alums are always doing this) in a new entrepreneurial scheme.

In the last few years, Gregorian chants have been rediscovered by the general populace, a trend that did not go unnoticed in the Boynton household in the Litchfield County town of Salisbury. Sandra figured that she could make her own contribution to rediscovering a musical heritage. She called Fenno Heath, the retired Yale music professor and Glee Club director. And together they produced a compact disc, not of Gregorian chants, but of pig grunts, using the "language" of Pig Latin—a barnyard amusement.

The satiric *Grunt* has sold at least 80,000 copies. Even so, it is not necessarily the sort of distinguished achievement that will earn Boynton an honorary doctorate from her alma mater.

LET GEORGE DO IT?

For a very long time, the campus was exclusively reserved for the privileged class of the right hue and correct religious persuasion. Very few African Americans were admitted. And as for Jews, there was a quota, although it wasn't always acknowledged.

One who made it in under the quota system was a young man from Stamford. For Joe Lieberman, Yale was—as for so many—a life-changing experience. "So what do I mean by that?" the U.S. senator asked rhetorically in the way politicians ask questions. In short order, however, he warmed to the nostalgic task.

He remembers A. Whitney Griswold—"a wonderful Yale name"—who was the president when he arrived "and a great proponent of liberal education, who said that the faculty wasn't there to teach grammar to grammarians or business to businessmen. It was there to teach the liberal arts, the accumulation of the Western civilization experiences and values.

"But the other thing he told us was that we should see ourselves as members of the democratic elite—with a small 'd.' For one reason or another we had made it to Yale—and what this meant was we had a responsibility to give back, to contribute in whatever form we chose to do so."

It was at Yale that Lieberman got his first real taste of public controversy. As editor of the *Yale Daily News*, he took part in the tradition of holding a weekly press conference with the school president, who by then was Kingman Brewster.

"I had a kind of a run-in with him," the senator recalls, a "real learning experience." In 1963 the Yale Political Union invited Alabama governor George Wallace to speak. Students and members of the New Haven community protested the appearance of a blatant racist. "Kingman Brewster was convinced that the speech would be a threat to public order." But Lieberman wrote an editorial in favor of the visit.

"I wasn't fond of Wallace. What he had to say was obnoxious. But this was a university community; we couldn't be in the business of suppressing unpopular opinion." This led, inevitably, to a confrontation with Brewster at the weekly meeting. "We tussled. This was a moment of testing. In the end, I think he had a grudging regard for what I did."

As it turned out, Wallace never came to campus.

Senator Lieberman remains a big fan of the Kingman Brewster administration. It was Brewster, he points out, who opened the campus to women and to African Americans and West Indians. His patience and persistence was a lesson for anyone with an interest in politics.

CALVIN NO. 2

I met Calvin Hill at the athletic director's office. He was there, visiting from his home in Virginia, to give a speech and to accept the Walter Camp Football Foundation's Man of the Year Award.

Despite his impressive accomplishments, Hill is not among the most famous of Yale grads—indeed, he may be known to younger folks only as the father of Grant Hill, an NBA superstar. But there was a time for the dad, and we recalled it.

First, he saw a painting in the A.D.'s office that drew his attention. "Frederic Remington," he pointed out as he walked over to carefully inspect it. It reminded him of all the Charles Russell etchings he once found in the hallways.

Calvin Hill did not make his fame locally as an art connoisseur. He was one of the best football players that ever played The Game against Harvard or any other Ivy League opponents, the man Carm Cozza (his retired coach) thought could have started at any position, not just running back.

Hill was at Yale during years of turmoil, when students were fighting for civil rights; as a black student, he was in an awkward position. Students were also protesting against the war in Vietnam. Hill's hero during that time was Rev. William Sloane Coffin, the pacifist and professor. "I wanted to be like him," said Hill, and in fact he made plans to become a minister. What he became instead was a very prominent Dallas Cowboy.

After our chat, Hill was introduced to an assembly of Yale athletes. He told them that as a young man he had intended to go to UCLA, to play in the Rose Bowl, but there was something about Yale that drew him.

He learned a good deal in the classroom and joined in the routine standing ovations for certain professors. But the learning also extended to the field in a way well beyond the intricacies of football.

Hill told the joyous (and painful) story of the 1968 season, when Yale was the champion of the Ivy League. He recounted the last difficult minutes of the final game of the season, which was, of course, against archrival Harvard, played that year in Cambridge. Yale was ahead 29–13 with less than two minutes to go. But Harvard staged a remarkable comeback. In short order, the Crimson scored a touchdown and a two-point conversion. Then, trailing by only eight points, Harvard recovered its onside kick. The Yale defensive players seemed exhausted and panicked as Harvard marched down the field in the final seconds.

Hill and Brian Dowling (the team's quarterback, who was later immortalized as B.D. in Doonesbury) had an urgent suggestion for Coach Cozza. As clearly the best players on the team, they volunteered to go in on defense. They believed they could stop Harvard. Cozza suspected that they were right, but he didn't send them in. If he were to do that, he explained, the kids who were replaced would always remember that the coach didn't have confidence in them.

And so the game played out the way it was meant to. Harvard scored another touchdown and two-point conversion in a miraculous (from its point of view) turn of events. The next day the *Harvard Crimson*, the school newspaper, printed the legendary headline "Harvard beats Yale, 29–29!"

Hill and his teammates were, at the time, deeply disappointed. But the lesson he learned that day transcended the effect of any football score. He'd have never learned it at UCLA, Calvin Hill knew. Nor would he have met, that very day of the Harvard game, a wonderful young woman who eventually turned out to be Grant Hill's mother.

He took the lessons he learned at Yale and forged a fruitful and rewarding life, which now extends to working as a drug and alcohol counselor and applying his skills to aid troubled professional football players.

But for all his accomplishments, Hill retains a special affection for the four years he spent in New Haven, which to him will always be *the* hot Ivy League school. "One thing I'm most proud of," he told the assembled athletes so eager that day to hear advice from an old pro, "is that I attended, and graduated, from Yale."

Part Four

INNOVATORS

Speechless: Sol LeWitt's Silent Night

Never Show a Piece to Your Subject Before It Is Printed—a necessary and troublesome rule in journalism (though it protects a writer's and newspaper's credibility, it can seem haughty and unnecessary). It is a rule I made an exception for here. I hadn't intended to write about Sol LeWitt's seventieth birthday party. I have known him as a very private man. Moreover, I was a guest, not invited as a reporter. But when the event turned newsworthy, I was faced with a quandary. Afterward, Sol's wife, Carol, said, "You've got to write about this." Even so, when I finished the piece I felt I owed Sol a phone call to explain my intentions. "What?" he asked incredulously. And, "Why?" I told him that the decision was instinctive. He said, "Do you always act on your instincts?" I hardly knew what to say. Then he went on, "Well, if you wrote it, the least I could do is read it." I figured I had nothing to lose. The piece probably wasn't going to be printed anyway, so no rule would be broken. A few weeks later, I talked to Sol. I told him that I had decided not to publish the piece. He said, "Why not? I thought it was good." So I changed my mind again. (Originally published January 1999)

The hundred or so folks who filed into the Avery Court of the Wadsworth Atheneum one September night did so with a sense of suspended belief. They left a few hours later, shaking their heads, wondering if they saw what they saw and heard what they heard. Or, more precisely, if they didn't hear what they didn't hear.

And some left thinking that a hundred years later people would talk about this night at the museum in the same way some remembered the Paper Ball held February 15, 1936 (by evening's end, many of the revelers jumped into the Baroque-style pool), or the opening of Gertrude Stein and Virgil Thomson's stunning *Four Saints in Three Acts*, with its all-black cast, on February 7, 1934, another triumph of the legendary museum director Chick Austin.

The problem is that when you're in the place at the moment something propitious happens, you don't think of it as history in the making. This late summer night in 1998 was, even if it wasn't intended to be and wasn't announced in grand headlines in the newspaper.

After all, it was just a birthday party. That's all that Carol LeWitt intended for her husband, Sol. Earlier in the day, she had awarded him her private gift: seventy shares of common stock in the Cleveland Indians, Sol's favorite baseball team since his days growing up in New Britain. (Every other kid rooted for the Yankees or the Red Sox, and Sol, initiating a lifelong trend, decided to be different.) Carol arrived at the number seventy logically: one share for each year of her husband's life. This gift he accepted graciously. But would he actually climb into the family van and allow himself to be driven 35 miles up the Connecticut River Valley to the Atheneum on some trumped-up agenda, all the while suspecting that there might be a surprise party in his honor? Not likely.

For Sol LeWitt has at least two widespread reputations. He is at the very top of the contemporary art world, one of the leading innovators of conceptual art and later someone who defied categories as a creator of beautiful, innovative images. He has had installations and exhibits of wall drawings, sculptures, and other works in many countries.

Also, Sol is a notoriously private person, an extremely modest man whose picture does not appear in newspapers and magazines because he steadfastly refuses to participate in the rituals of celebrity. His idea of torture is standing amid people who talk about things that are meant only to be seen. Of course, the folks who came on this night were friends, and Sol is very tolerant of friends, particularly if they can recite the career win-loss record of Hall of Famer Bob Feller (266–162).

Awaiting the birthday boy, some of the guests sipped white wine and watched a video of Sol's mural (*Wall Drawing No. 793C*) being installed in the museum lobby in 1996 or a video from 1973 in which Sol's quotes on conceptual art (e.g., "Conceptual artists are mystics") were sung to an array of familiar tunes.

Guests who did not watch the videos simply speculated on how Sol would react to the evening's program. "I'm surprised he's coming," observed one museum regular. He asked me if I was there on business. No, I replied, just to enjoy the festivities and to help pay tribute to a friend. But as the evening wore on, the pen and pad came out.

Word spread that a busload of folks had arrived—a charter from Manhattan of some of the art world's biggest names. "Is that Chuck Close, in that wheelchair?" someone asked. Close is famous for his monumental portraits, which are re-creations of Polaroid close-ups. They have been described as both "intimate" and "colossal" and are all the more remarkable considering how they are made. In 1988 Close suffered a collapsed spinal artery and was paralyzed from the shoulders down. Despite regaining only partial use of his arms, he has continued to complete huge and intense portraits. Naturally, Close drew a crowd, and a proper suck-up receiving line was formed, which I joined.

We also spotted Robert Mangold, another giant of contemporary art. And there was Carl Andre, the minimalist who became famous and infamous hereabouts as the artist, or (some critics would have it) perpetrator, of *The Rocks* (formally *Stone Field Sculpture*), the $87,000 installation of boulders many years ago next to Center Church, across from the museum.

Finally, the guest of honor arrived with his wife. He appeared, against widespread anticipation, in good spirits. It was true, after all, that no matter what happened on this night, the Cleveland Indians had clinched a playoff spot, so how bad could life be?

Soon everyone was seated, partaking of native mesclun greens with house smoked shrimp, and then grilled chicken breast with wild mushrooms and lavender jus. But before the guests could get to their hazelnut dacquoises, Peter C. Sutton, the Atheneum's director at the time, strode to the podium and took off and put on his glasses in that suave way of his. He began his speechifying, which he does pretty well. He is a tall, distinguished, white-haired man, which counts for a lot. And it helps, too, to have something to say.

He said that Hartford could boast two of its sons among the great artists of their centuries (Frederick Church in the nineteenth and Sol LeWitt in the twentieth, for indeed, despite New Britain's claim on his childhood, he was born in the capital city). Sutton went on to say that there were some folks (including Close and Mangold) who wanted to offer a tribute to Sol on this auspicious occasion.

It was then that an odd thing happened. Sol LeWitt, who almost never speaks in public, stood up. The man who has so little use for words that his autobiography contains not a single paragraph but instead photographs of objects and important people in his life actually made a speech. It consisted of two words: "No speeches."

Sutton pressed on, thinking Sol was just being jovial and modest. But the artist stood up again. "No speeches," he repeated. "I don't want any speeches," he said, in case Sutton hadn't gotten the message. The director was beginning to get a little ruffled. "But people have prepared for this night."

"No speeches" came the call again from the head table. Guests around the room whispered and giggled and were aghast. They didn't know what to make of it, except that if Sol was making this effort to say something, he must be serious. Sol is not one to take lightly.

Folks at the Guggenheim Museum know that. When they asked him to be part of a monumental show on the history of abstraction in the twentieth century, they came away disappointed and so did he. No, he wouldn't participate in anything sponsored by the tobacco giant Philip Morris, which, to Sol's horror, also supported Senator Jesse Helms, a powerful enemy of artists. Sol once told the CEO of Honeywell that he had to decline a large commission because the company makes munitions. When the CEO asked the artist to reconsider, Sol asked the CEO if he would reconsider the idea of producing what he produces. Sol also turned down a commission from Nestlé because that company promotes its baby formula in Third World countries instead of encouraging breast-feeding.

In short, this is a man who makes sacrifices for what he believes and who thinks that when everyone is doing things a certain way, it is time to take a different path.

"Well," said Sutton, "how about just one speech?"

"No," asserted the artist, ignoring pleas by friends at the table.

"But it is to be given by Andrea. It's a roast, too."

Andrea Miller-Keller, who had been curator of contemporary art at the museum, was Sol's champion there for more than two decades. She had known him from the days when, on Hester Street in New York, his style of living was so sparse—or, to employ an art term, minimalist—that he had two spoons, two forks, two cups, and one pair of shoes. She cheered him when the Museum of Modern Art hosted his first retrospective there in 1978. She curated many of the shows from the LeWitt Collection, a part of which Sol intends to donate to the Atheneum.

She also was the one who nearly two decades later proposed to the Western Hemisphere's largest art festival, the Brazil International Bienal, that a LeWitt wall drawing be the featured work. São Paulo newspapers, in reviewing his piece there (*Wall Drawing No. 808*), referred to Sol as the major living star of the Bienal. Andrea now intended to give an informal tribute.

She had written this speech for his birthday: "I have felt privileged to watch your life unfold over the past few decades, from

Hester to Chester. There were the pre-Carol days, when less was more. And then there was the remarkable blossoming (and major expansions) of the Carol days—a burst of color in your work, enduring love, home, daughters, animals, nannies, properties, bat mitzvahs, philanthropy. There was even arranged by you, the man who doesn't drive, the very touching surprise arrival of a BMW sedan in your driveway on the morning of Carol's fortieth birthday." Andrea had more, too, but got to say none of it.

As Andrea rose from her chair and began the trek to the podium, Sol said, "Come here." She did as told, warily. "Let me see what you've got," Sol commanded. She gave him a piece of paper on which she had made notes. He put it in his pocket. "I'll read it later," he said.

Andrea went back to her seat, confused and feeling a little awkward, but also realizing that Sol was never a man to be pushed around by large institutions or by friends. Besides, she could take comfort in her long history with him.

Still, there was a buzz around the room. This was, in large part, a group of artists. Would they stand, or sit, for this? No.

Carl Andre, the rock man, rose from his place at a rear table. "No artist in the world has done as much for other artists as Sol LeWitt," he said, referring to Sol's patronage and support of those who are struggling and developing. Sol's impressive private collection includes many works by artists who needed a sale. He also helped them in other ways—paid their rent, or quietly helped pay their kids' tuition. Sol often complained to museum officials that they shouldn't waste money on openings of exhibits, feeding and wining people who don't need to be fed and wined. Instead, museums should be buying the work of starving artists.

The crowd loved Andre's tribute and applauded, for indeed Sol and his wife, Carol (the founder of Ceramica, with stores in Italy, Connecticut, New York, and Colorado), are among the most thoughtful and generous of spirits. A host of charities are beneficiaries of their largesse. And Carol's work on behalf of the Atheneum as a trustee was tireless. Sol himself is a rare combination for an artist: independent and intensely interested in the public welfare. Yet even this wouldn't go down on such a night.

Sol would accept no praise. He simply motioned Carl Andre to sit down and announced, "This from the man who 500 yards from this museum has the greatest public art installation in America."

He was referring, of course, to *The Rocks*. *The Rocks* would be celebrated that night. Sol LeWitt would be celebrated suitably, perhaps in a hundred years (he'd be 170 years old, with a commensurate amount, we presume, of Cleveland Indians stock, and by then would cheer the Tribe's first World Series title since 1948). In 2098 they'd recall that Atheneum night so long before, the night when the greatest conceptual artist invented a new way to say "I love you." By showing up and shutting up.

Everything's Coming Up Rossi

It's easy to pitch a profile of an artist to a magazine editor, as long as you gird yourself for rejection. Art is indispensable to life, but it doesn't always sell magazine copies. On the other hand, when I suggested to Charles A. Monagan, the editor of Connecticut *magazine, that I undertake my first piece for him by writing about artist Karen Rossi, he was all ears. This was partly due to the way I made the pitch—careful to insert the phrase "$50 million in sales last year," a sequence of words not often connected with artists. (Originally published May 2002)*

One spring day, an art consultant for United Technologies Corporation explored the old factories along the Windsor Locks Canal in search of talent and opportunity. When she arrived at the building on the far end, she noticed the warnings at the entrance to Karen Rossi Metal Sculpture: APPOINTMENTS ONLY. NO SALES. PUBLIC NOT ALLOWED. BEWARE OF DOG. THIS IS A CLOSED STUDIO. THIS PLACE IS MY HOME.

And she knocked.

The BEWARE OF DOG sign was not for effect. A sixty-five-pound bundle of determined energy named Brindle, half pit bull and half (well, what does it matter?), lunged at the inside of the door and, while revealing a perfect set of incisors, made it clear that the visitor was not on the day's agenda. Still, the consultant persisted, and one of the workers muzzled the dog, let the visitor in, and brought her to meet the boss.

Karen Rossi's day had been occupied, as customary, with a variety of tasks in her 10,000-square-foot space. She applied the final touch of blue paint to a small metal representation of a sailor—a model to be reproduced by the thousands for the U.S. Navy. She supervised work against a tight deadline for a greeting-card design to sell to C. R. Gibson in Nashville. She made plans, for an upcoming New York Gift Show, to meet with the company that licenses her whimsical sculpture. She attended to the production details of large fabric banners, the sale of which would benefit the United Way's September 11 Fund. She reviewed her pitch to Hartford Hospital as a contender for a commission that would be the centerpiece of the new lobby. She prepared descriptions of pieces she would display on an hour-long QVC show. She considered the agonies and expenses of protecting against copyright infringement (knockoffs of her pieces were beginning to appear in the marketplace). And she was telling me, for the purposes of a profile about an artist-as-business-whiz, how a little girl from South Windsor who simply yearned to "make things" grew into a woman whose work is sought around the world.

The visiting art consultant interrupted this full agenda, identified herself, and stated her mission—trying to hook UTC up with local talent. She asked Rossi, "Could you tell me about your work?" I remembered the bountiful years when UTC proved a generous benefactor to Connecticut artists, and I thought, "Bingo!

Good for Karen. She'll consider the visit a great opportunity."

But the consultant never had a chance to finish her pitch. Rossi told her, "You can see what I do on my Web site. If you're interested, you can reach me then." The interview was over. The woman left a card and said goodbye. I would not have anticipated such a scene, or such a switch—the artist rejecting the corporation.

I have known Rossi for many years. There is no one more cordial to deal with or—the signs on her door and Brindle notwithstanding—more warmly enthusiastic. When I was *Northeast's* editor, she often e-mailed or called with ideas for community projects. But, as I learned, Rossi is not naive. She possesses a business sense that ought to make UTC chief George David sit up and take notes.

To spend any substantial time with the visitor, as Rossi explained, would have been wasteful. The consultant was clearly not informed and was fishing for a deal. Rossi has no patience for that—the days are long past when she had an uncertain sense of the value of her time. Moreover, all her energies are now channeled toward what must be done to keep a fast-growing enterprise healthy and expanding. In short, there isn't a moment at the epicenter of whimsy to indulge in foolishness.

This was one of the ironies I observed over the next several weeks as I explored the qualities that have led Rossi to Neiman Marcus and to boutiques at Bloomingdale's, to hundreds of shops in this country and abroad, to hospitals and other community institutions that seek and display her work. And to what eventually led to the licensing of an enormous array of miniature mobiles, clever flying characters (crafted in China and trademarked as "Fanciful Flights") complete with tiny charms and narrative tales, all packed neatly into clear plastic Chinese takeout boxes. There is Java Junkie, Bathing Beauty, Mr. Fix It, Wild Bird Watching Woman, Barbecue Man, Zelda the Jungle Shopper, and a variety of mermaids. In all there are about 400 amusing representations selling from $20 to $35 each that, if the present course plays out, will add up to $50 million in sales in a year's time. And this line represents only a part of her enterprise.

How to explain the emerging phenomenon that is Karen Rossi? There is no shortage of eager volunteers. John Boyer, director of the Mark Twain House in Hartford (beneficiary of many of her efforts), says that she creates "some of the last things you'd expect to get out of metal—a sense of delicacy and fancy." Her longtime friend from New Orleans, potter Lucianne Carmichael, says, "She expresses in her art that down-to-earth life energy in all of us with her silliness and with her vigor." Linda Simpson, vice president of product development at Silvestri (Rossi's licensing firm), says, "It's the right timing, and timing is everything. People now need to feel good, and Karen's work makes you smile." Debra Lynn Porter, a New York importer, says, "I think that most adults, myself included, take life too seriously, forgetting what it was like to be a child. Look at one of Karen's mobiles, and in one second you are instantly transported to the land we adults can only dream of—a land all lucky children live in."

So who is Karen Rossi, meddling in the dreams of childhood but nobody's pushover? Or, as Porter describes her, "the world's muse—charming, alluring, playful, witty, knowledgeable, insightful, smart, classy, grounded, and beautiful."

What if we used metal to interpret the artist in her late forties and created our own mobile of a flying Karen Rossi? She would have long, flowing hair and a brilliant smile that suggests her staccato laugh. Charms (she calls them "visual logos") would include dogs, paints, hiking boots, cans of cranberry juice, a travel guide, keys to Connecticut cities, and perhaps a copy of *When Bad Things Happen to Good People.*

For all of the amusement they provide, Rossi's sculptures have a complexity that may not at first appear obvious. As many of those who know her metal sculpture and her life will point out, artists don't learn to sell $50 million worth of work overnight, and they don't do so without paying a heavy price.

Would any of Karen Rossi's success have happened without the ordinary and extraordinary twists and turns in her life? If her mother hadn't plied her with early stories of living across their Roxbury street from the great sculptor Alexander Calder? If her father hadn't quit his secure position as a foreman at Pratt & Whitney to build a welding business out of his garage in South Windsor? If Rossi herself, who up to fifth grade had been one of the most popular girls at Eli Terry Elementary School, hadn't been ostracized the following year for sticking up for a classmate—an act that sent her off, alone, to find solace in her artwork? Who can accurately pinpoint the origins of inspiration and necessity?

There is no doubt that strong will and sacrifice were consistently present. "My parents were always very supportive until it came time for college. I wanted to study art. They wanted me to go to a state college and would pay as long as I studied anything else." Art, they argued, is a fine hobby but not a living. "I was mad at them." So she went off in a huff to Massachusetts College of Art, paying for the first year with her own savings. "Then I ran out of tobacco-picking and babysitting money and couldn't support myself living in Boston." She finally acceded to Alva and Margaret Rossi's wishes, enrolling as a foreign-language major at Southern Connecticut State University, a "prudent" path that soon led to big trouble.

"I was bored at Southern. It was awful. So I convinced a guy to marry me. And that was even worse. He was a nice guy, but I needed to make things—we were too young for this, and I didn't know how to balance marriage and belief in my artwork." When the marriage ended after only two years, Rossi used her waitressing skills to finish at Southern, hoarding hours for drawing and printmaking, her media at the time.

Her tenures at New Haven restaurants turned out to be time well spent. At L'Aventura she cooked tableside for high-profile regulars, from Channel 8 personalities to Bart Giamatti, then president of Yale (who brought literati with him and spoke to Karen in perfect Italian), to Paul Newman and Joanne Woodward.

"I had been shy. More than that, I had grown up very poor in a farming town and never experienced anything like this," Rossi remembers. "These people had money to spend on wonderful wine and food. And I was able to talk to them—to present meals to them with expertise." All the time, she was drawing on certain pictures from her own childhood: Sunday-night meals of homemade tortellini. Every artist—it is a rule, isn't it?—must wait tables. But in Rossi's case, it was an experience that boosted her confidence and gave her a sense that she could survive in elite and educated circles. "It brought me out of the shadows."

Careers begin at such moments—when you're doing something else. When you're stealing whatever time you can to work on your art, and then someone asks you for a piece for a show. "How about making the herald angel Gabriel?" they ask. And as a result of your "loose" religious upbringing, you respond, "Who's that?"

It could have all ended there. But Rossi instinctively forged ahead, as she did later when she was asked to produce menorahs for synagogue gift shops. Hanukkah became a private miracle of light.

Influential people were learning about her. Robert Gregson, the urban visionary and creator of public art projects, saw Rossi as a community resource. In 1985 he chose her for a public project that brought large pieces to troubled New Haven neighborhoods. Gregson recalls, "Karen's project was the first completed—a whole series of flying people spinning around in the breeze. Karen was unknown at the time . . . but even then she inspired everyone. The city came out with trucks to help in the installation. The neighborhood had a party for the unveiling, with punch, balloons, and even the mayor came. It was a wonderful launching for Karen, and so typical of what happens with her."

Her career path from that point may seem glamorous to the casual observer. One-of-a-kind pieces began to command prices ranging from $100 to one for $35,000, and Rossi moved her studio from her father's garage to her own space in Windsor Locks, employing several people to help. Her work was becoming well known locally, and she received a variety of commissions and many honors—among them being named the first artist in residence at St. Francis Hospital and Medical Center in Hartford.

Rossi's St. Francis connection has been intimate. She worked there with terminal patients, teaching the techniques and rewards of making art. One of the patients was an interior designer who, with Rossi's inspiration, transformed her drab hospital room into a beach scene using props and posters. Millie Prayzner, nurse manager of the oncology unit at St. Francis, remembers that it allowed the patient "to have control over her final days." Rossi's work at the oncology unit hit home when her thirty-two-year-old cousin Lisa became terminally ill. After Lisa died, Rossi felt compelled to produce a gift for the hospital (which she says came from Lisa), a representation of angels "because Lisa always said the staff members at St. Francis were angels."

These compulsions were typical of Rossi. Beneath all that whimsy was a frenzy, something that drove her to the point of exhaustion. Pam Aselton Croft, her friend since childhood, recalls that Rossi always worked late into the night, even on school projects. "I still worry about her health," Croft says. But the demands of metal sculpture—a tedious and labor-intensive process—were overwhelming. Money was always an issue. Raw materials were expensive, there was a payroll to meet, and there wasn't time to both produce a large body of work and market it adequately. Even as word of Rossi spread, she was becoming more and more isolated. Her life was her work: long hours creating the pieces, and then trudging off to trade shows in New York and other places, heavy metal in tow, with every minute spent displaying, selling, networking, and fretting about where the next dollar would come from.

At such shows Rossi would be buoyed by remarks she heard about her pieces. "People in the aisles were saying, 'It's so Chagall-esque.' I didn't even know Chagall's work very well." And she was thrilled to get a big order from Neiman Marcus. But when Bloomingdale's went nuts over her stuff, she had to refuse its overtures. She'd already committed to a competitor. What kind of career is this if starving artists feel obliged to turn down big checks from Bloomie's?

There was consolation, though, in the form of a private life that could finally be called by that name. Until then, as her friend Lucianne Carmichael put it, "Guys always broke Karen's heart in one way or another, because she gives herself so completely, always thinks the best and thinks it's all going to work." Or, as Rossi herself confided, "I do a lot of eclectic things, extremes. I go to Europe and ride third-class because I can ride on the wooden seats. I would take these fellows who live in New York on camping trips [which didn't have happy endings], or guys who would go camping but aren't comfortable in a tuxedo."

Then Rossi began dating a jewelry artist named Denis Perlman, of Northampton, Massachusetts. He was tall, fit, curly haired, and, as everyone described the MIT grad, generous in spirit. They took long walks together and climbed mountains. They flew in his small plane, a Mooney, to Cape Canaveral and Martha's Vineyard, and to meet his sister, Cindy, in West Paris, Maine. Cindy, who had always been protective of her brother, was overjoyed by the match. "Karen was open and loving," she told me. As for her brother, she could discern his feelings. "Denis said a lot with his eyes."

Perlman encouraged Rossi to get her work out to more people. She got similar advice from Paul Brent, of Pensacola, Florida, an artist she met in 1992. "I had begun licensing my work and told her about it," Brent says. He explained to Rossi the process of licensing—giving a manufacturer and marketer the right to reproduce a prototype and sell it in exchange for a small percentage of the gross sales. In short, you do the work once instead of over and over again. Thomas Kincaid, a painter, has made his worldwide reputation that way. Others such as Mary Englebreit and Bob Timberlake have prospered as their signature styles show up on coffee mugs, dolls, rugs, and place mats. But Rossi was a sculptor. How could that work?

It could work if fate intervened. Linda Simpson was the Bloomingdale's buyer who had been turned down by Rossi. Later, when she became the vice president of product development for Silvestri, a company that seeks artists and licensing opportunities, she remembered Rossi. She offered the chance Rossi needed.

But even this promising turn of events required adjustment and sacrifice. For one thing, the contract with Silvestri offered her no advance payment. It was based on a percentage—a one-digit percentage—of total sales. It would take months to receive any royalties. Rossi also felt that she had to advise regular customers not to order one-of-a-kind pieces because soon they could purchase similar items at much cheaper prices. In short, income was drying up even as prospects for sales increased. Rossi was four months behind on the rent for her Windsor Locks studio. For a while she even considered going back to work as a waitress to help with cash flow. Worse yet, the commitment she needed to make to Silvestri got in the way of her romance with Perlman.

Their relationship was not simple. Rossi recalls, "He was ahead of me in age, and in business. He was secure, and I wasn't. Though we wanted to be together—Denis wanted a family and so did I— we had conversations with no answers." It didn't help that Rossi, without the clear prospect of substantial income, was traveling extensively. Perlman was supportive of this but frustrated, too.

As other trade shows loomed, Rossi and Perlman reached a crisis point. He kept calling, but she didn't return the calls. She felt pressured, uncertain of what to do. They hadn't spoken in weeks when, in January 2000, she flew off to Atlanta, and then to Dallas, complete with costumes and high hopes for her new line. From Texas she called to hear her messages. Among them was the surprising and wonderful news that Silvestri sales had jumped by leaps and bounds, much more than anyone expected. But what would that mean for her? She needed some expert advice, some clarity.

She called Perlman, but there was no answer. She left a message on his cell phone. Then she called Blair Dalton, her bookkeeper—perhaps she could advise. The conversation, however, was not at all what she expected. Blair asked, "Have you heard about Denis?" Rossi had heard nothing, though it had been all over the news in New England. One of the region's finest artists, while landing his own plane in a fog in South Carolina, had crashed. Denis Perlman was dead.

Rossi flew back from Dallas immediately in a state of shock. She and Pam Aselton Croft took a long walk in the freezing rain. Cindy Tinsley, Denis's sister, her own sense of loss overwhelming, comforted Rossi, who was filled with remorse over having cut off communications. Even now she says, "You can't not talk to people. You never know what's going to happen. I still have a ghost feeling—as if he is going to call any minute."

Time, work, and nature proved therapeutic. Walking in familiar fields one day, Rossi saw a hawk and was convinced it was Perlman. She told the hawk about the payoff at Silvestri and all the other successes.

Perlman would be pleased that she has been able to purchase a lovely old house in Norfolk, not far from a place that her parents own. And that, if reluctantly, she has finally entered the ranks of consumers (though her friend Pam is obliged to advise her on what to buy at the mall). Rossi finally is free of concern about a roof, a square meal, and health insurance.

Still, even with tens of millions in sales, she has not yet had the time to build real financial independence. Moreover, current success, as brokers like to say, is no guarantee of future success. Fueled by financial anxiety, she has learned that to leverage her brand—to make herself what she's always wanted to be, the Martha Stewart of the art world (without the criminal record)—she has to be as successful with other products and licenses. That's why she's working with Bernina, the sewing-machine company, on designs for embroidery and with Toland (a banner company) and United Design (a resin company). Even so, she has trouble sleeping at night.

"It's very frightening," she says, "to learn about artists and business." She reads everything she can about how artists succeed and fail. She wonders how people make millions and then lose it all. She knows the pitfalls. "Managers who took a high percentage. Deals with hidden expenses. Artists have a demanding lifestyle. You are on the road, spending a lot of money, a lot of money is swirling around you. You know you've earned it, because you've been slaving from day one. But it takes a lot to keep the whole operation going."

It doesn't help when counterfeit mermaids and other Karen Rossi–like figures show up in certain shops in New England. Rossi had to hire a Hartford law firm, Cummings & Lockwood, to protect her intellectual property rights. Though no lawsuits have yet been filed, the expense and aggravation sometimes consume her.

She finds comfort in friendships. Cindy Tinsley is astonished that she still hears from her late brother's flame. Rossi has only to ask to get Tinsley's ear. And the artist finds solace where she has always found solace—in the studio. "If I didn't make things, I would fall into depression," she says.

Still, she would forgive me if I complained that she is a little too close to this to appreciate all she has done. She remains a rare spirit and inspiration. Robert Gregson says, "When I think of Karen, I think of Katharine Hepburn—that fierce independence, that belief in herself." She is an exquisite model for all who would presume to make art.

She is also a list maker—she has to be. So I asked her to make one for me, of "the secrets of your success that can be passed along to anybody who wants to be an artist." We repaired to her studio's lunch room, where she dictated the following:

1. Unconditionally love what you do. Try to look at things in positive ways, though it's not always easy. At the end of every day, I always try to figure out what I can do better.

2. Think systematically. Follow up, and call people back. Say thank you. Be meticulous: In art, if you make this incredible piece and you don't take a picture of it (before it's sold), it doesn't exist.

3. Don't take no for an answer if it doesn't feel right. Many times people said something couldn't be done. As an artist, people don't take you seriously because it's not a "real" job. You've got to teach them. Creative problem solving and creative thinking are what artists do. Some guy on a plane told me a bunch of excuses about why his company was having problems. I'm always thinking about solutions.

4. Trust your intuition. Have faith in yourself. You're the only

one given this unique set of tools. And trust their worth and their effectiveness in the marketplace, even if your mother says, "What?"

5. Protect your mental, physical, and spiritual well-being. It's tough to get rest when your mind won't shut off. My Karen Rossi Wellness Program involves doing something that's easy to put off: making a doctor or hair appointment, riding my bike in the basement, or calling an old friend.

If there were a sixth point, from all appearances it would have something to do with canines. As Rossi finished her list, her studio was alive with the rituals of Brindle and also with Shep, the one she calls "the hopeless Lab." It was also humming with the sounds of employees engaged in a variety of tasks. Many are college students who earn money between semesters and who draw knowledge and inspiration from Rossi. There are also two much older people who work for her.

These would be Alva and Margaret Rossi. Karen says, "My dad never tells me he's proud of me. But he tells his friends. And that's enough for me."

EPILOGUE

Karen Rossi ended her relationship with Silvestri, the licensing company. Since, she has taken on several partners, each of which specializes in new lines (fabric, note cards, calendars, etc.). A lawsuit against the company that was making knockoffs of her sculpture ended in a settlement in Karen's favor. Her present schedule includes more time for commissions. She completed a sculpture in honor of the birthday of Stanley Greenberg, an author and political consultant (as well as Congresswoman Rosa DeLauro's husband). And she accepted a commission to do a large piece for the new Evergreen Mall in South Windsor. Karen's personal life has changed, too, and for the better. She and her fiancé, Greg Pasborg, a wine consultant, live in a house on a lake in Meriden. She says Greg is what she's not—methodical. "He helps me slow down, and this helps me keep my balance."

Arts, Ideas, Madness

When I am considering possible subjects to write about, administrators don't emerge at the top of the list; it is never my intention to put readers to sleep. But if accomplished people are willing to provide colorful and candid stories about how things get done against overwhelming odds, well then, the idea does go to the top of the list. (Originally published June 2004)

With the announcement that the 1995 Special Olympics World Games would be hosted not in some exotic capital but our very own New Haven, a pervasive Yankee attitude quickly emerged. A major daily newspaper predicted across its front page that as a result of the Games, highway traffic would suffocate the state. "*Please*," the paper seemed to be saying, "take your big idea somewhere else, and don't bother us with it."

At the same time there was, and remains, another prominent mind-set common to all Connecticut cities. Case in point: I talked to a Litchfield County couple who followed their Mark Twain fanaticism to the ends of America—driving their Winnebago along the Samuel Clemens Trail from his woodsy birthplace in Missouri to Virginia City, Nevada, to every other spot where the legendary writer spent significant time. I asked them, in light of their extraordinary 8,000-mile journey, how Twain's nineteen-room Victorian palace in Hartford stood up against all they had seen. They confessed that they had never visited the house, just 28 miles from their own, where their literary hero lived for seventeen productive years and where Huck Finn was born. "Go to Hartford?" they seemed to be saying, "How great can an attraction be if it's in Connecticut?"

Such attitudes were prevalent when three New Haven–area women came up with a new and ambitious plan in the wake of New Haven's Special Olympics World Games (which, by the way, caused no significant traffic problems, though it drew large crowds). Anne Tyler Calabresi, Jean Handley, and Roslyn Milstein Meyer had the idea that since the Games had brought such positive attention to the city, the momentum should continue with something bold and expensive.

Calabresi in particular pleads guilty to the charge of obsession, illustrating what righteous indignation can do. She calls herself "an old radical"—one who rails against social inequality, lack of opportunity for inner-city children, and the burgeoning violence in our world. Yet from her earliest memories of growing up in the environs of New Haven, she saw the city's ability to lift its residents. At the tender age of seven, at the Shubert Theater, she watched as the grace of the Ballet Russe de Monte Carlo brought her mother to tears.

Children of New Haven in the present era grow up with much different images. So, against a backdrop of widespread drug dealing, and at a time when the city's mothers feared letting their kids out into the streets, Calabresi created youth athletic programs.

This led her, Meyer, and others to found LEAP (Leadership, Education, and Athletics in Partnership), with the goals of training a new workforce and drawing employers to New Haven. This, in turn, inspired another grand vision, another way to address economic stagnation. She and her cohorts would create for their city what Calabresi had seen in Italy and in Charleston, South Carolina—a world-class arts festival. A way to focus on the assets of a special destination.

In doing so, they could also address the frustrations and opportunities that result from their city's diversity. So many ethnic neighborhoods—Ukrainian, Italian, African-American, Latino, etc.—and no significant way to bring them together. Also, there was the usual suburban fright. Calabresi couldn't persuade her Woodbridge neighbors to drive downtown, despite its prominent cultural jewels, for fear of something dreadful happening to them.

But Calabresi kept seeing the possibilities. A billion-dollar infrastructure was already there—historic buildings and a gorgeous town green ringed by elms and lamplights. "We didn't have to dig the lake to have the regatta. This was a case of the *Emperor's New Clothes* in reverse."

With Handley and Meyer, she began planning for the first International Festival of Arts & Ideas, with multiple events on multiple days, much of it free to attendees. "Everyone," Handley says now, "thought we were crazy. They patted us on the head." Many festivals of lesser scale had been tried and failed; how could something on a much grander scale succeed? But the naysayers did not understand the capacities of these women, who came of age in the workplace in an era of glass ceilings, and who developed along the way the moxie to persist and succeed.

Jean Handley had become the first female vice president of SNET, prospering through optimism and quiet determination. Calabresi (an anthropologist) excelled at persuading others, and Meyer (a clinical psychologist) was the community consensus builder. Working from office space SNET lent them, they raised money and got residents and institutions (including Yale University) enthused about bringing a world of entertainers and thinkers not only to perform but also to venture into the city's neighborhoods as messengers of hope.

Calabresi said she was ignorant about how to do such a thing. "But it was like going into a forest and picking one flower, and then picking another," until she had a spectacular bouquet.

Handley researched the weather—many performances would be outdoors. The founders circled June as the ideal month, before Tanglewood and other performance competitions. Climatic data showed the third week as the month's driest period. Weather history, of course, is one thing. Mother Nature laughs at this, and these days thunder occasionally competes for attention with big-name acts.

The festival runs sixteen dry and wet days. In 2004, its ninth year, 275 events in 50 venues around the city and in satellite locations drew about 150,000 people, including suburbanites who were impressed by the quality of the festival—and by the crime statistics over the first eight years, which drew a total audience of more than 800,000 people. Number of cars broken into: zero. Number of purses snatched: zero. Number of Calabresi's unattended umbrellas stolen during rainstorms while their owner wandered from the green to other events: zero.

There have been, obviously, many performance highlights. Fitting right in with the theme of Connecticut's inferiority complex is this one: Michael Frayn's play *Copenhagen* had opened in a small London theater and was scheduled to move to the more commercial West End. In the meantime, the script was sent to the three founders of the International Festival of Arts & Ideas and its then–artistic director, Paul Collard. They all read and loved it, though its "action" was just three people talking in Denmark about the idea of a nuclear bomb. It was entertaining, important, and, considering that the festival was still young at the time (before its annual budget rose to $3.5 million), inexpensive to produce. So they booked it. When the *New York Times* got wind of the success of *Copenhagen* in London, a reporter called the West End to get tickets there. She was told it wasn't in the West End yet—but if she wanted to see it, she could take the train from Grand Central Station to New Haven. The reporter responded incredulously, "New Haven! What the hell is it doing *there?*"

One little miracle builds others. The Metropolitan Opera. The Royal Shakespeare Company (which did its part to enliven the local economy—many actors came into the Edge Tattoo Co. to decorate their ankles). The Saigon Water Puppet Theatre. A conference on governance and corruption (always timely). Little Richard. Strange Fruit. *Alive from Palestine: Stories Under Occupation* (not without attendant controversy). Kool & The Gang. Gilbert & Sullivan. Street Cirkus Frank. At the heart of it all—*A Midsummer Night's Dream.*

Mary Miller, the second artistic director (imported from Great Britain), told me that the three founders have pulled this off through "unflinching passion for this city, their vision of empowerment through the arts, and extraordinary pragmatism."

For the three, after all their success, certain images stand out from the very first festival. On the final night, a crowd of perhaps 25,000 (no real way to count) came to the green to hear a concert by Ruben Blades. Calabresi saw all city and suburban neighborhoods represented, and, as the night progressed, many people dancing. When it was over, she watched as everyone carried picnic baskets and folded lawn chairs back to their cars. There was a natural glow over the city she has always loved, and she decided that she had peacefully died, and that this was Heaven.

Miss Alyce at the Tap Room

Every community has its legendary characters, and they are attractive subjects for the writer. But rather than simply sitting down with them and having them tell me stories, I prefer to watch them in action, as here. That way I can immerse myself in the subject matter and, when ready to write, can weave the past and present. (Originally published January 1997)

Well, of course, there are the girls. They are here on weekday afternoons, fresh from school, their books and coats in the hallway, their tap shoes on. The girls wear leotards, or at least a few of them dress that way. Some of the slightly older ones wear sweatshirts that say 101 DALMATIANS or UCONN HUSKIES or JUST BE HAPPY, which makes Miss Alyce a tad unhappy. She tells her students, "You wouldn't go to a soccer game dressed like a dancer." Yet there is no malice in Miss Alyce's reproach; there is no malice in this studio, nothing but a certain gentle persistence. There is an idea—Miss Alyce's idea for all of thirty-five years of teaching—that each child, gifted or not, can find a sense of satisfaction and self-expression on the well-marred oak floor. A friend of the dance teacher describes her this way: "charismatic, with the distinct ability to make people feel good about themselves."

That is clear enough. Girls of all tender ages seem to adore her. So do the adult women, up to age seventy-seven (at last count), who see fit to try their toes at tap or the other varieties of dance in her West Hartford studio. And we're not even talking yet about Miss Alyce's most unusual clientele, whom we will eventually consider: people of a different gender who never in their most distressing nightmares thought they'd wind up in a chorus line.

But it is instructive first to watch the Thursday afternoon girls as they line up against the wall before taking their turns doing "flaps." To mere pedestrians this is a fancy prance, a "brush and a step," where the dancers scoot across the floor, hands by their sides. "Good," Miss Alyce tells one young charge. "Better," she tells another, because indeed it was better than the time before. "Keep your feet closer to the floor," she advises another. You can see in these little girls a great variety of attention, responsiveness, and self-confidence. You can see in one young face an eagerness to be at the front of the line, to show the others what she can do. You can see in another face, hidden partially by a hand raised to the mouth, the uncertainty of youth.

You can see a certain concentration in the "triplets," when the children tap, tap, tap with the right foot and then tap, tap, tap with the left, moving backward across the room, their arms extended for balance, an attempt to keep the rhythm steady. "I must do this right," you imagine girls saying to themselves. "I can do this right." For what you sense in this place is a feeling of safety, of relief from the ordinary rigors of childhood and adolescence.

When she teaches the girls their tap lesson and demonstrates the steps, Miss Alyce wears her own dance outfit: black and sleek and, perhaps, very much like the outfits she wore so many years ago as an innocent in Manhattan when she first caught the eye of Joe DiMaggio, Liberace, and Sammy Davis Jr. She remains the same striking dancer who for two decades taught the virtues of ballet and tap and jazz and Broadway dancing to the girls of Miss Porter's School. But it is easy to get ahead of yourself in this tale. It is part of the eagerness with which anyone would want to relate the story of Alyce Carella.

In the faces of little girls today you can see the possibilities, and you can see a world open to them, a much different world than when Alyce was growing up. In the years after World War II, there was opportunity aplenty for men. But for a little girl the world was not quite as wide and inviting. In the two-dribbles-and-pass era, when perspiration was considered unladylike, any sensible father would want for his daughter a normal path to success; that is, "Dear, it's always good to know shorthand."

How is it that a child in such an age when there are no role models can know right out of toddlerhood that she wants to be a dancer? And can't be talked out of it? By the time she was seven, Alyce "ate, slept, and drank dance. I would perform for people at bus stops. My mother was so embarrassed." Alyce watched movie or stage musicals and when she went home tried to duplicate what she had seen. When she was an adolescent, she took a bus—actually two buses—from West Hartford down to Franklin Avenue and Barker Street in Hartford to Patti Ann Rita's studio. Of her teacher, she recalls, "She was such a beautiful person, enthusiastic and energetic. I wanted to be just like her."

Which is not to say that Alyce's father, loving though he seems to have been, wanted her to follow in Patti Ann Rita's inspired footsteps. "My father was concerned that I could make a living out of something he considered a hobby." Never mind that Alyce's grandfather had done well with the clarinet and was a longtime member of the Hartford Symphony. When Alyce's father insisted she take a job as a legal secretary, she secretly snuck off to Arthur Murray's; it was two weeks before her dad found out she was teaching dance. When her father insisted, upon Alyce's graduation from St. Joseph's Academy, that she enroll in college locally, she became, at age seventeen, a babe in New York.

You might imagine a different Manhattan of the time, but it was no less busy and no less eager to take advantage of an unworldly, not to mention considerably attractive, teenager from West Hartford. You might imagine her first audition, at a supper club, with Alyce pretending she was twenty-one and getting away with it. And soon thereafter finding herself in the chorus line, having a fine time performing, until the strap on her shoe broke and the shoe went flying off into the smoke-filled air and landed precisely on the dinner plate of Georgie Jessel. This comedian knew an opportunity when he saw one and invited the young dancer to his table. Jessel was the first star she had ever met. But there were others. Buddy Hackett noticed her, too. She was struck that Jessel and Hackett wanted to know all about her. Well, it doesn't seem surprising, does it? Why wouldn't they? What they learned, and what all the men learned, was that dancing—not "old" men, no matter their achievements—was what interested Alyce.

On the other hand, Liberace had a different interest. "A most charming man," Alyce recalls. "Elegant on stage, in love with his red suede loafers, and always genuinely loving life. He would rehearse and say, 'Girls, what do you think of this?' He was asking advice of us amateurs." Sammy Davis Jr. always knew what he wanted to do, including introducing young Alyce to her first limousine equipped with a bar, telephone, and television.

But the figure she remembers most from those days is Joltin' Joe, and the portrait she paints is of a lonely DiMaggio. This was in the days after his marriage to Marilyn Monroe ended, when he was coming at night to the 500 Club, sitting there quietly, shyly, and taking an interest in Alyce. The innocent she was, Alyce had very little idea of his enormous athletic accomplishments. She saw only a sweet gentleman who made a good friend and, in the kitchen of the club, a fine batch of marinara sauce. You can imagine the two of them at the table, one whose whole life had been baseball and who had been the object of adulation, and the other whose life was just beginning.

Alyce's father could imagine it, too. Joseph Carella finally decided that this dance thing couldn't be all bad, not if he could come down to Manhattan to meet the great Joe DiMaggio.

In fact, when Alyce returned home to West Hartford and opened her first dance studio, Joseph became just as supportive as Alyce's mother had always been. At the first recital of her dancers at the Bushnell, he strutted around the lobby with a flower in his lapel.

This, then, is not really a story about tap, or even about how Alyce took Miss Porter's by storm and spurred the renovation of the Play Barn into a wonderful dance studio. Or about many other accomplishments, including bringing up three children (from a marriage that lasted but a few years), or about turning out many professional dancers who later opened studios of their own ("I've created my own competition!" she'd claim). It is really about fathers and daughters, about what happened in the years after Alyce's father recognized the value of what she does, and how Alyce turned that recognition into a phenomenon.

Maybe you've been there and you know. Maybe you've gone down to Bulkeley High in Hartford on a June weekend to see the annual recital of the Alyce Carella Dance Center, and you've seen what happens there. The many ensembles of girls, of course, do their ambitious routines in gorgeous outfits. But it is not the girls, however talented, who make these recitals newsworthy.

At one such recital, Miss Alyce looked out into the appreciative audience and on a whim said, "You know, dads, I'd like to see you up on the stage." There was, not surprisingly, a catcall or two and no immediate volunteers. But a few months later, she had an idea. She had always taught mother/daughter tap. Would father/daughter work? Would fathers be interested, or would they remain more comfortable accompanying their boys to football games? Alyce tacked a signup sheet to the bulletin board and a few days later saw forty names.

It is January 1997, and we are back in the tap room. Across the hall Alyce's daughter, Laura, is teaching Broadway dance to the usual suspects, but here there are seven men for the Tuesday night class, men in tap shoes who, by and large, you would not mistake on the street for dancers.

Rich Jahne, of Wethersfield, warns me, "You won't see too many Fred Astaires or Gregory Hineses tonight." On the other hand, this veteran of Miss Alyce's class and recitals tells me that no matter the level of their achievements, they will no doubt get a grand reception in June at Bulkeley High. Time has proven that the dads merely have to strut out on stage in their white ties and tails, or whatever costumes are chosen for the night, for the audience to erupt into applause.

The applause is only partly for the level of fancy, or semifancy, footwork. It is also because the dancing dads have made this very public commitment to themselves and to their daughters. Dancing is important, a point the fathers are making by their participation. Dancing is something they and their daughters can do together, something they can be proud of together, something that will engender pleasant and lingering memories for decades.

On this night in January, long before the recital, Miss Alyce is putting together a routine for the men, and they are doing their best to follow it. They are doing a "lunge" and a "shuffle ball change" and "triplets" and "flaps" and "scuff" and putting them to music. She tells the men that the general theme for this year's recital is the calendar, and that she is thinking of tunes that would fit that theme. Can anyone think of some? I suggest "April in Paris" or "September in the Rain," or "June is Bustin' Out All Over" or "Will You Love Me in December As You Do in May?"

These men have their own calendar comments. Considering the intensity of tonight's rehearsal and the difficult steps Miss Alyce clearly wants them to master, they collectively worry that Miss Alyce's expectations might be a little high at this early moment. "This is January, not June; don't push us too hard," one dad says.

But Miss Alyce keeps them involved in the planning. She tells them that she has a tune in mind for them, a Father's Day tune for when they dance with their daughters, if only she can find a version of it that isn't "too bluesy." It is the Cole Porter song "My Heart Belongs to Daddy."

Such a selection would be fine with Rich Jahne. After nearly a decade of tap dancing with his daughter, Robin, now sixteen and "a little too tall" to be his regular partner, he knows that his time on the floor with her is limited. He says, "I know she'll have a new partner before too long. Still, on her wedding day, Robin and I are not going to dance to 'Daddy's Little Girl.' We're going to do a tap routine."

The Heart of Town

*Ralph Waldo Emerson wrote that nothing great was
ever accomplished without enthusiasm. He was certainly
right. When Clinton built its new library, it seemed
clear that the effort was the result of a handful of people
who just wouldn't say no. And part of their inspiration,
I was sure, came from a member of the library staff.
The journalistic challenge was to show that enthusiasm,
not merely to point it out. (Originally published October
1998)*

As shoreline towns go, Clinton, though lovely enough, never
enjoyed the tony reputation of two neighboring communities. As
the saying goes (there are variations), "Guilford has the culture,
Madison has the class, Clinton has the clams." A clever little put-
down. But even in staid old Connecticut, times and perceptions
can change. Look at little Clinton now.

Here you can go to the opera every August at the handsome
town hall auditorium. You can visit a vineyard any time of year.
(Chamard, owned by the Tiffany & Co. chairman, produces prize-
winning wines.) You can stroll Fifth Avenue, as in Saks Fifth
Avenue, at Clinton Crossing, the shopping mecca that brings in

hefty tax revenues. Or you can visit a handsome new attraction that will make you warm all over, even though there are no winter coats for sale.

We are about to enter the new version of the Henry Carter Hull Library, where there are many stories to tell, and not all of them on the shelves. There is "The Mouse That Laughed" and "The Bad News about *The Bad News Bears*" and "The Secret Quilt" and "The Great Girls' Bathroom Transformation" and even "Things about the Itsy Bitsy Spider We'll Bet You Didn't Know."

To get to the heart of the place, which is, according to those who know, an actual person (a woman with bright blue eyes), you must park in the lot that has room for seventy cars and walk to the front door, where—in this converted bank building—there is still a slot for a night deposit.

We begin, though, with a mouse—one that has proven to be an elusive creature. We are not in the office of "the heart" of the place, but in the office of "the brains." Gary J. Cummings, the head librarian in this town since the late 1970s, is pasting peanut butter to an old-fashioned mousetrap. He explains that he has to resort to the old ways because the Havahart trap is apparently ineffective. The offending mouse must have giggled as he purloined the bait and ran off to eat his dinner amid, we presume, the Agatha Christies.

It is an annoying, even embarrassing, problem in the office of the chief of such a splendid building. But no building, new or old, is immune from such creatures, and Cummings goes about his mouse catching in good humor. It is such a small matter. All in all, his office, resident mouse or not, is a vast improvement. No longer does the director work in a basement the way he did when the home of the Henry Carter Hull Library was that lovely but cramped old building on Main Street.

I am in Cummings's presence not for mouse chasing but to ask about one of his employees, Lynn Hidek, the children's librarian. I met her a few days earlier at the ribbon cutting. She was the one wearing an unobtrusive suit of bright yellow; she didn't seem to worry that she would stand out that day in the celebratory crowd.

"Best decision I ever made," Cummings says about hiring Hidek in 1986 over five candidates who, on paper, were better qualified. Each possessed a master's degree in library science, and Hidek had only her bachelor's in elementary education and experience at a day-care center. Recalling that time, the director says, "Lynn walked in the room and filled that room with her personality, her exuberance, her optimism. I thought, this is the person I want."

He figured that if she would agree to get her master's degree in library science, the school could teach her how to catalog. But no school can teach personality or the ability to inspire children.

The lights are out. It's not the new library's fault; the whole block seems to have lost power. Hidek addresses the twenty-five children in this morning's story hour as they file into the reading room. "We don't need lights," she says, and indeed they don't in this naturally bright and airy place.

The power outage, however, reminds her of another time, back in the old building. There was a brief outage there, too, after a summer storm hit the town and made it impossible to draw water from the wells. Hidek came to work without the benefit of a morning shower and was uncharacteristically tense.

There was lots of activity at the old library that day, including a book sale intended to be outdoors. The storm put an end to that, moving the sale inside and making for a pretty crowded building. Hidek's group of children was scheduled to see a film. It was a movie about baseball that she borrowed from the Middletown library service, but in doing so she broke a rule: "The eleventh commandment: Do not show anything you haven't previewed."

The Bad News Bears sounded innocent enough until the first four-letter words emanated from those cute little creatures on the screen. The kids in the library loved the movie, but Hidek was jumping out of her unwashed skin. The place was crowded with adults, including a woman known to have highly protective attitudes about children. When, at the end, Walter Matthau poured the champagne for his little champions, Hidek sort of sank back and prayed for the day to be over.

She makes too much of it, of course. Children, even at a tender age, are subject to worse, even at home. But Hidek prides herself on a certain attitude about the library—that it is a haven, that it is a safe and wonderful place to introduce children to ideas and attitudes not easily available to them in other ways. It is never too early, she argues, to expand a mind.

So here is what happens when a baby is born in Clinton: The baby and its parents are immediately eligible for the "Bright Beginnings" project, a brainchild of Hidek.

"I always want to lure, to invite, to cajole, to force every parent into the library," she says. Many parents weren't read to as children and don't understand the value of it. And so Hidek found some grant money from an organization that has, as its goal, the prevention of child abuse. She acknowledges, "It would be foolhardy to think that bringing a child to the library will prevent child abuse, but this place does provide an extended family to parents. If parents are struggling, we can provide support."

When a member of the children's room staff sees a birth announcement in the paper, parents are invited in and gifts are given. There is a book for parents about what to expect from a baby in the first year. There is a gift for the baby—its first volume, a heavy cardboard book that can be gummed or pointed at. "Let's get them right at the beginning," Hidek says. There is also a refrigerator magnet that has a place for the baby's picture and for the proud label OUR LITTLE READER.

My assumption—that Hidek's passion for getting children off on the right path is a legacy of her picture-book childhood—turns out to be a valid one.

Not that she had all she wanted. Lynn Rollo and her parents lived in a working-class East Haven house on a dead-end street. There, books opened a world for her. She remembers her introductions to these simple volumes, her "golden moments," as she calls them, when she simply took inventory of the library shelves.

She brings me a copy of *A Child's Garden of Verses* by Robert Louis Stevenson. "You know this?" she asks, explaining that her grandmother often read from it to her. I say that I know of the book, but when I think of Robert Louis Stevenson, *Treasure Island* comes to mind, and Hispaniola, which on this day is being threatened by a hurricane instead of Long John Silver. No, I don't think of "Bed in Summer," which (along with other verses) she can recite:

> *In winter I get up at night*
> *And dress by yellow candle-light.*
> *In summer, quite the other way,*
> *I have to go to bed by day.*

When Hidek makes plans for her story hours and orders books for the children's room, she remembers how, as a young girl, "I loved crying over the emotion of *Little Women*." And "When I read *The Diary of a Young Girl*, by Anne Frank, I was shocked. This little girl could have been my friend."

Hidek's childhood, in short, took her far from that working-class neighborhood and enriched her heart and her mind. This was the legacy that inspired her at first to become a teacher and then led her to Gary Cummings. Now she can hardly believe her good fortune. She is here, in her "dream job," in her "dream life." In the old building, her 3-by-5-foot office was a converted girl's bathroom.

Even before the new library opened, it was the scene of an honor for Hidek. When she turned fifty, the bank building was being converted into a $1.3 million example of community enterprise and vision. Her husband, Ed, had an idea for a library fundraiser. He would give Lynn a surprise birthday party, and instead of people bringing gifts, they would make a cash donation. It was, by all accounts, a wonderful event, attended by many townsfolk and old friends. Library board member Si Taubman, a major force behind the new building, recalls that the party was "an outpouring of love for her." It included the Hideks' grown children, Lori and E. J., performing a parody of their parents dancing the Monkey, complete with exaggerated facial expressions.

There is evidence of other tributes on the wall of the reading room, something also presented as a surprise. Lynn Hidek and other members of the children's staff were given a quilt that was a community project. It features dozens of squares drawn by alumni of the children's story hour, and it depicts scenes from their favorite books.

The whole of the beautiful Clinton library is, in effect, a tribute to Hidek and to other local citizens whose passion helped create the momentum that made such a building project possible when—after all, this is a town (though charming) like any town—there was once influential opposition.

We are in the reading room now, ready for the story hour. We are here with children ranging in age from three to four. Hidek is at the front of the room, where the quilt hangs and where she, with the help of a hand puppet named Carter (for the banker Henry Carter Hull), has just lit the story light.

She takes out a book. *The Itsy Bitsy Spider*. The kids are excited because they know the part about the waterspout and how the sun came out.

"But this is very tricky," says the librarian, as a little girl in red clings tightly to her mother's thigh and stares. "What's gonna happen next?" the librarian asks, almost breathlessly. You can see in her delighted face evidence of what she believes, that reading aloud to children offers one of life's great rewards.

You can see her beam when little Isabella, wearing a pink dress, raises her hand. "Yes, yes, Isabella," Hidek says, "you're right." The itsy bitsy spider turns out to be quite adventurous, climbing not only the waterspout but, as it turns out in this book, also the kitchen wall and the yellow pail, the rocking chair, and the tree. Each time, the itsy bitsy spider, to put it mildly, faces some difficulty, which it overcomes. A fine lesson for a child at this age. For a person at any age.

But if you think you know what happens here, you are wrong. Because there is always a surprise ending in a Hidek story hour. As she reminds me, the purpose is to hook the listener and to open minds to all possibilities.

Old MacDonald had a farm all right. And on that farm he had a pig, and a cow, and a duck, and according to little Isabella, "sheeps." But did you know that Old MacDonald also had a Martian?

With a beep-beep here and a beep-beep there, we enter a place that reminds us each in our own way of how the wonders of the world, how our own golden moments, first made themselves known to us.

EPILOGUE

In 2004 the Henry Carter Hull Library was named the seventh best library in the nation for its population size by Hennen's American Public Library Ratings. Director Cummings and the staff were suitably proud of this achievement. Then, in March 2005, the library and town of Clinton suffered an immense loss. Gary Cummings died awaiting surgery after suffering a heart attack. He was fifty-two.

The Colors of Home

A famous play and movie suggest that there are six degrees of separation. I am not a math expert, but I believe that the odds of finding connections are even cozier than that. The world is a small place, and everywhere you go, there is a story to tell about home, if you keep your eyes open. (Originally published January 2005)

In the public squares of the walled city of Lucca, Italy, large posters announce two January performances: MOMIX, DANZA, TEATRO GIGLIO. 28, 29 GENNAIO 2005.

I point this out not to suggest that you book a flight to Milan and then a puddle-jumper from there to Pisa. And from there to a rental car, qualifying you to take your life in your hands on the Autostrada to Lucca. All of this to support the innovative dance company based in Washington, Connecticut, and founded by the brilliant Moses Pendleton. You could have certainly caught the scheduled program—*Sun Flower Moon*—more economically at the Warner Theater in Torrington.

Still, you'll agree it makes more sense to use Lucca rather than Torrington as a base to illustrate the worldwide influence of Connecticut artists. Though every June the world of arts (and ideas) comes to New Haven, the favor is returned many times over the rest of the year. A fact that is largely ignored.

The chatter in our coffee shops over the winter is far more likely to be about whether George Steinbrenner will exact his revenge on the Red Sox (I certainly hope not) and far less likely, for example, to be about how the Japanese and French compete to lure the eminent alto sax player, Jackie McLean, from Hartford's north end. And only subscribers of Dave Brubeck's newsletter out of Wilton, where the pianist/composer and his wife live, know that last spring in Naples, Italy, there was "a small riot outside the theater because [Dave's] concert was not open to the public."

Who among us has celebrated that there is but one stage company in the world that has performed on all seven continents? Though I am a longtime fan of our National Theatre of the Deaf, I admit that the seventh requires an asterisk. David Hays, the company's founder, held a workshop aboard a boat in Antarctica, which he argues counts because there are no cities in Antarctica (only official outposts).

Speaking of the stage, how can we measure the effect of the late Arthur Miller's work worldwide? Years ago, *Death of a Salesman* had its debut in Shanghai. Even in China, where there hadn't been a legacy of road men who survived "on a smile and a shine," the climax of the play hit audiences hard.

Many other longtime Connecticut residents join Miller in the state's universal legacy: Of course there are Philip Roth and William Styron, whose novels have been translated into many languages, as have the stories of Wally Lamb. Add to that the poetry of James Merrill, Robert Penn Warren, and William Meredith;

Leonard Bernstein's music; Meryl Streep's riveting characterizations; Roger Tory Peterson's depictions of our natural habitat; the histories of William Manchester and Theodore H. White; Marian Anderson's angelic voice; Garry Trudeau's biting wit; the architecture of Cesar Pelli and Philip Johnson; the screen triumphs of Ron Howard and Paul Newman; Robert Motherwell's abstract expressions; Maurice Sendak's world of imagination; Katharine Hepburn's . . . well, Kate.

It's an old story that a prophet is never a prophet in his own land, but among Connecticut's creative thinkers, there are exceptions. The artist Sol LeWitt, who lives in Chester, has been celebrated widely in America and even, when unavoidable, in the state of his birth. (When UConn deliberated a few years ago over whom to offer a major commission, it was a woman from Turkey who made the winning argument for a new LeWitt.)

His retrospectives in San Francisco, Chicago, and New York drew hundreds of thousands of visitors (including me to the last two). The *New York Times* art critic called the Whitney exhibit "the most beautiful" show to hit Manhattan in recent memory.

Over the years, I have visited Sol's studio many times to watch the master at work. His new ideas at an age (mid-seventies) when many are content merely to recall old ones sends an inspiring message to anyone who paints or writes or otherwise creates something out of nothing in the hopes the work will resonate with the public.

One of the things that caught my eye was an intricate design in pencil, obviously meant as a plan for an enormous piece—another huge wall drawing, the form for which he is so well known. But not exactly. Sol explained that the plan was for *Whirls and Twirls 1*, for the ceiling of the public library in Reggio Emilia, Italy.

That he had such an opportunity was not surprising. He has received commissions all over the world. Italy, where he owns a home in Spoleto, displays a great deal of his work. Every major museum sells copies of a lavishly illustrated book that shows the locations of LeWitts from the Italian Alps to the heel of the boot.

I had imagined—anybody would, looking at those plans for Reggio Emilia—that it would be a grand thing to see the work when it was finished. Italian ceilings in public places are, of course, historically something more than coats of white house paint. Moreover, I would have the rare opportunity of inspecting a completed work before the artist saw it. If you know Sol's method, you know that it is to design projects and then hire young artists to complete them—just as an architect would leave the actual construction to builders.

But seeing the finished product was, for me, a long shot. I hadn't been to Italy in thirty-five years, and even that was a drive-by. Besides, I didn't have to travel that far anyway to see Sol's magic. All I had to do was go, as I do regularly, to Congregation Beth Shalom Rodfe Zedek in Chester, where he designed the sanctuary's bold ark in the shape of the Star of David. Or to the Wadsworth Atheneum, where his work (including a new wall drawing) is represented widely, or to the New Britain Museum of American Art.

But fate has a way of intervening. And in this case, family connections allowed us to rent a spacious apartment for a bargain rate in Lucca, not that far on the map from Reggio Emilia. Lucca is where we saw the Momix signs, and from where we set out on day trips along the Connecticut Art Trail, Italian-style.

The first sojourn was to Reggio Emilia. I looked on the map

and saw that from Lucca the most direct route was through mountain passes, a trip that seemed as if it would require an hour or so. We were to meet with a specially arranged guide in Reggio Emilia at about 1:00 P.M. But at 3:30, we were still driving the rented Citroen around hairpin turns, and we had no cell phone to call and say we'd be very late. It was not our intention to play the role of ugly Americans. Without exception Italians had been cordial to us, even when our attempts to speak their language fell short. Still, without a way to communicate, we were frustrated. And when we finally arrived in the city, our tardiness was compounded by parking too far from the center of town.

When we finally reached the center of town after a hurried hike and turned left toward the library, or *biblioteca*, we stumbled on an antidote for alienation and tension. Large posters outside the library entrance displayed bursts of familiar, intense bands of colors: red, yellow, blue, orange, green, and purple. Sol LeWitt's colors, the comforting colors of home.

Our appointed guide for the tour had long ago gone home, so we wrote a note of apology and left it at the desk. Then we went straight to the reading room, the site of the new work. Dozens of young people sat at desks, concentrating on their books. By contrast, we were transfixed by what was above—more than 60 square meters of intricate combinations of, well, whirls and twirls, in bands precisely 8.5 centimeters wide. Or what the book published in conjunction with the piece refers to as a "polychrome kaleidoscope." But at the moment, no words came to us except, "Do you have a hanky?"

A few days later, we visited Spoleto and saw more colors of home. A cafe displayed LeWitt tiles. At an elegant restaurant, the waiter proudly told us about two celebrities who have been customers, Sophia Loren and Sol LeWitt (although never at the same table).

The next morning, we toured Spoleto's contemporary art museum. A room is devoted to the late Roxbury sculptor Alexander Calder (displaying the exchange of letters concerning the huge public piece that Calder created for the city). Another room is devoted to the colors of Sol LeWitt.

The woman who guided us through the museum that day asked where we were from. We said Sol LeWitt's town, Chester, Connecticut. She was delighted. She said she spent four years in Chester, working for Sol. "Say hello," she said, "to Sol and Carol, and to Enza at the post office, and Peter and Jan, and Michael and Dina and their new little one, Scarlett. Oh, Connecticut is such a beautiful place."

Part Five

JUSTICE RAINS

Femme Fatale

At the time of this highly publicized murder trial, in early 2002, I had no media outlet. I had left the Courant *after twenty years and was yet to sign up as a regular columnist for* Connecticut *magazine. I was drawn to the trial nevertheless. Its circumstances seemed sad and yet universal. And, instinctively, I knew that someday I would write about it. For the time being, though, I was mere spectator in the courtroom—witness to an attempt to apply a standard of justice to a sordid and grotesque matter. (Originally published October 2002)*

The second most talked about murder trial of 2002 came to an end in August. I missed the sentencing—the day Judge Robert Devlin Jr. peered over his eyeglasses at Beth Carpenter and informed the thirty-eight-year-old lawyer that she would spend the rest of her life in prison, without hope of parole. Still, from several trips to New London's criminal court during the testimony and final arguments, I pictured the startled reaction of a most unusual convict.

In some ways, murderers are all alike: violators of an ancient commandment and, within our borders, the penal code (53a–54a) of the Connecticut General Statutes. Beth Carpenter, then, is no different from Michael Skakel, who was convicted earlier of the murder of Martha Moxley in Greenwich and who led in the headline count, or from the people with less impressive pedigrees whom public defenders try desperately to keep from death row.

And yet, in the years since she committed her crimes—through her fugitive period; through extradition from Ireland, where she had sought asylum; through the trial itself—Carpenter developed an outsized reputation. Regardless of whether it ultimately could be proven that she was guilty of capital murder and related crimes, she was certainly guilty of first-degree manipulation of men.

The key question before the jury was this: Did Carpenter's former boss and lover, Haiman Clein, act on his own behalf or at Carpenter's request when he hired a hit man to kill her brother-in-law, Anson "Buzz" Clinton III? Clein, who admitted his crime and was in prison awaiting sentence on a plea bargain, was the chief witness for the state. The torrid Clein/Carpenter affair was no doubt one of the public draws.

The courtroom filled each day with trial junkies and reporters. Several people talked of producing books from the proceedings.

As a story of criminal conspiracy, it is more than a little odd—usually it's a rival lover, not a brother-in-law, who becomes the target in such affairs. (It had been Carpenter's position, in the midst of a fierce child custody dispute, that Buzz Clinton was abusing her then three-year-old niece, Rebecca, an accusation that was never proven.)

Odd or not, there was a broad obsession with the case and more than enough drama to make a book. Even the courthouse hallway provided usable scenes. Dee Clinton, mother of the victim and a hallway denizen, offered nonstop commentary and the contents of a bottle of "Anti-Bullshit Pills" to witnesses who were about to testify and to Carpenter's chief defender, Hugh Keefe. Clinton referred to the lawyer as "Sunshine" in something of a derisive tone. One morning, as he often did, he asked Dee Clinton, "How are you today?" She replied, "Armed and dangerous."

When Keefe first spotted me in the hallway, he said, "Would you like to meet my co-counsel?" He led me to a small conference room where Tara Knight was sitting with the defendant. I shook Knight's hand. I had no choice but to shake Beth Carpenter's as well and say, "Nice to meet you." What else can you say to a woman charged with murder? I did not ask the questions I was thinking: "Why do you wear skirts with slits up the side to court, and why do you flip your fiery red hair in that suggestive way?" It was not hard for me to imagine Haiman Clein, more than twenty years Carpenter's elder, doing his own kind of flip over his hot new junior associate, particularly in his state of heavy drug use.

People ask me if Carpenter is exceptionally pretty. I would not say so—there is a hard look about her. Yet there is no denying her sex appeal. On this issue, jury members wouldn't require five minutes of deliberation. They could see it in her sway. They could see her attempts to make eye contact, though I never sat close enough to report whether she focused only on the men. I noticed that she scribbled notes on a yellow legal pad, as if she were earning $250 an hour instead fighting the battle of her life. From what I could observe, she seemed satisfied with her defense team.

Hugh Keefe is one of the best trial lawyers in the state. He has a strong courtroom presence—the same gift of Irish gab and the same mop of intensely red hair he had in the early 1980s, when he sat at the Yale Bowl with Austin J. McGuigan, then the chief state's attorney, and other courtroom foes to ostensibly cheer the Eli eleven, but really to just enjoy a few beers with the boys.

The jury was no doubt impressed by Keefe, at first. He was far more humorous and engaging than prosecutor Kevin Kane (himself an alumnus of McGuigan's tenure). Kane, whose gray suits are understated and whose hands are almost always in his pockets, gives the impression he's stumbling for something to say. But veteran courtroom observers compare him to Jonathan Benedict, Michael Skakel's prosecutor, in terms of tenacity, patience, meticulousness, and brains.

Keefe was unfailingly sarcastic in his questioning of hostile witnesses such as Haiman Clein. Using the usually respectful address "Sir," as if he were saying, "You dirty lowlife," he asked: "Now, sir, is it a fair summary that you were using cocaine, alcohol, and Xanax at the time of the murder, sir?" and "Is it true, sir, when you were trying to impress Beth Carpenter you didn't want her to know you were looting clients' funds, did you, sir?" I didn't count how many times Keefe used the word, but it reminded me of an eighth-grade history teacher who kept saying "at any rate" so often that I began to keep count in my notebook.

Clein, providing the only hard evidence against the defendant, should have been an entirely impeachable witness—a once prominent lawyer who descended to murder, thievery, and drug abuse. But on the stand, the sixty-one-year-old Clein, burly and weighted down by the prospect of a sentence (yet to be pronounced) that could be forty-five years, was low-key, remorseful, and surprisingly believable. About cocaine, he said, "It affected my judgment in certain personal matters, that's for sure." About his future, Clein lamented, "I don't expect to get out of jail, no." With such a witness, Keefe's ridicule seemed to backfire. The jury, on the other hand, listened carefully to Kane and came to appreciate his straightforward (if decidedly more boring) approach.

At various points in the trial, neither Keefe nor Kane could anticipate testimony or jury reaction. One of these times was when the judge ordered the man who had actually pulled the trigger to testify. Mark Depres was shackled, driven from the prison in Newtown, and escorted by two guards through a courtroom door that only the bailiff could open. Dressed in his inmate's uniform of green overalls, Depres looked as if he had not cut his hair for a year, and he wore a disdainful look on a face that, by comparison, would make Hannibal Lecter's seem downright cherubic. The judge asked the former Deep River resident three questions, including whether he understood that his plea bargain arrangement (which, like Clein's, was intended to avoid the death penalty) could be voided if he didn't tell the truth. Depres's answer to all questions was stone silence. He would not, it was clear, live up to his plea agreement. He would be, on this day, practicing for not guilty by reason of insanity.

It was generally thought in the spectator rows that the trial was up for grabs—until Keefe put his client on the stand, a move that surprised veteran court observers. She answered most of his questions about events from long ago with precision and denied any part in the murder. When prosecutor Kane's turn came, Carpenter remembered almost nothing, including the answer to the question of whether, standing out in Clein's driveway, she waved his underpants for his wife to see. "I don't recall" didn't seem to satisfy such an inquiry. The jury was onto The Great Manipulator. The sexy, vulnerable, forceful, helpless defendant. He wouldn't say so in the hallway, but I think that Keefe counseled that she not testify. Carpenter, whose ability to manipulate had, for the most part, gotten her out of scrapes in the past, must have insisted.

Guilty. Guilty. Guilty. On all three counts, the jury said—the most serious counts on our books. Saved only by an extradition agreement with Ireland, where there is no capital punishment, that the death penalty wouldn't be sought. Beth Carpenter tugged at Keefe's right arm, a gesture both to steady herself and to lean one last time on her defender. But even she knew that she was out of real options. Within hours, she would trade her slit skirt for drab prison garb. There would be no talking, or manipulating, or flirting her way out of this one.

Free At Last. Almost.

I have followed the work of the novelist Wally Lamb from the beginning. I published his first short story in Northeast, *and a few after that. Moreover, all of us at the magazine celebrated his success on* Oprah *and the best-seller lists. When Wally ran into serious trouble with the state of Connecticut, it was only natural that I would weigh in, particularly because I saw it as a clear case of censorship—and of punishing Wally and his class of inmate writers for the crime, as I saw it, of telling the truth. The case eventually had a satisfying outcome, but not until well after this piece appeared; there was much posturing and pain in the interim. (Originally published July 2003)*

In late January 2003, Nancy Whitely drove from her rented house in Monroe to the Danbury Fair Mall, thinking all the way, "What does a guest wear to the *Today Show*?"

Clothes have always been problematic for her, as she had indicated in her tightly crafted memoir, *Orbiting Izzy*. About preparing for a job interview a few years previous, she wrote:

"Nervous about my hair, I had settled on a slicked-back French twist. I put on a stolen Liz Claiborne suit, stockings, matching maroon pumps. 'Be brave,' I muttered, and faced the mirror. Bleached blond hair, green eyes, long legs, huge breasts: I'm one of those girls who looks slutty no matter what I wear."

Slutty would not do for an appearance with Katie Couric in front of a nationwide audience. Whitely had to look respectably tailored, and for a price that a part-time deli clerk could afford. At H&M, she found a brown suit with elbow patches: the literary look. This time she paid for the outfit and for the matching pumps and purse; no more theft for her.

A few days later Whitely and her boyfriend, Dave Csey, took the Acela from New Haven to Manhattan at the expense of a media giant. They were given a room at the Omni Hotel, at a rate considerably more per day than the $110 or so it had cost the state to incarcerate Whitely during her term at York Correctional Institution in Niantic, a consequence of credit card fraud.

She could hardly believe her good fortune. Just a couple of years earlier she had been in despair—taking the blame, rightly, for terrible things she had done to herself and others. Now she would be a toast of the town.

One of the New York stops was NPR. As with her television appearance, Whitely would be joined by her mentor, novelist Wally Lamb, who had worked with her and many other inmates at York in a writing workshop. Out of that workshop came a series of excellent memoirs, which Lamb and HarperCollins put together in a book entitled *Couldn't Keep It to Myself*.

Whitely explained her background to an old bushy-haired man with a hearing aid who was also waiting to be interviewed. When she finished the story, he said, "I'll tell people I met you." Then she asked him his name. He said, "Norman Mailer." What an oddity—

the author who had championed the work of the notorious prisoner Jack Henry Abbott, and who himself had stabbed one of his wives, interviewed on the same day. Whitely said, "I'll tell people I met *you*."

The night before the *Today Show* was troublesome. Whitely couldn't sleep much. It was terrifying enough to face a national audience. And in her case, she didn't exactly exemplify ideal behavior.

Her life, until York, had been a mess. Worse, it wasn't as if she could blame society or her parents. In one of her stories, she had unflattering things to say about her mother and father, "but a lot of people had worse childhoods than I did. I was responsible for the things I did, not my parents. Alcohol, heroin—at $150 a day. I was stripped of everything." In Whitely's descriptive essays, self-loathing and despair are themes. When her mother succumbed to cancer, it seemed as if there was nothing to live for.

Then Whitely was sentenced to York, and the timing was right. The writing workshop taught by Lamb and Dale Griffith (a certified teacher), and sponsored by the state, changed her life and the lives of others.

Women in prison are experts at self-deception and lies. Suddenly, they were required to be what they never had been: honest. Lamb, who taught writing at Norwich Free Academy for many years before becoming Oprah-famous for *She's Come Undone* and *This Much I Know Is True*, insisted on this. Whitely says Lamb created a safe place. "You knew instantly he would never do anything to hurt you."

He encouraged the women not to write about their crimes, or they would seem to be profiting from their misdeeds and the state would take any money received. So they wrote instead about their early lives or the dehumanization of prison life. It did not occur to anyone that the state would intervene anyway.

As Whitely prepared for the *Today Show* in New York, she was concerned that Couric would ask questions about the Department of Corrections' civil lawsuit. Whitely had been advised by counsel to avoid answering such questions.

A sheriff had arrived at her door in Monroe with a subpoena. It announced that the state of Connecticut was suing to recover the $5,600 advance that HarperCollins had paid her and the other authors represented in *Couldn't Keep It to Myself*. The state could technically do so because, under legislation passed a few years before, the DOC could collect for the cost of incarceration. As a practical matter, however, the state has seldom pursued this course. There are about 19,000 people behind bars and 175,000 former inmates. Action has been brought in only a couple dozen cases— after windfalls from lawsuits, or inheritance, or lottery winnings. The DOC saw a windfall as a result of the York workshop. Never mind that the authors had donated part of their earnings to shelters for battered women, or that what they had left helped the ones who got out pay dentist bills or down payments on apartments, or buy an outfit that could be worn on fruitless job interviews.

The state didn't stop at the $5,600 advance. Katie Couric might ask about Bonnie Foreshaw's DOC invoice: $913,000, for accommodations since 1985. A television interview could be entirely consumed on only this topic: How could the state, which hopes to rehabilitate prisoners, punish them so severely for learning how to become a success?

Why did the DOC, and then Attorney General Richard Blumenthal, go after these women? They argue it's the law. But the law is vague and selective—and begs to be rewritten. They also say the women benefited from state-run programs, and the state should get the proceeds. Applying similar logic, then, should the state be liable to inmates and their heirs for programs that don't work and that contribute to recidivism, or suicide?

There are, of course, the concerns of victims and their families. Some activists have fumed that these women have profited in any way from their lives of crime. Whitely has sympathy for the argument. "If I had a child who was murdered," she says, "I wouldn't be too eager to help prisoners. But we're all in the same place. We all want to stop crime. Rehabilitation is one way." Burying heads in the sand won't accomplish anything. Consider that Whitely—with skills and three years of college—can only get a job making deli sandwiches. What about the people who get out with no skills, or who still can't read?

How much of this could Katie Couric ask in four minutes, the time allotted to the interview? When Whitely awoke from her fitful sleep at the Omni, she worried about this and about her feet, which had swelled. Her boyfriend had to cut a new hole in the shoe straps. Later, as production assistants applied makeup, Whitely felt on edge, "but it was a good nervous, not a going-into-surgery nervous." When a producer started talking to her and Lamb, it was decided that the four-minute segment would become seven minutes.

On the set Couric impressed Whitely with her sincerity. The author preempted any tough questions by admitting her culpability and also gave generous credit to others for her success. Couric praised Whitely's writing—and rightly so. For here is a deli clerk who has insight to human nature and a lovely narrative style, and who, with her cohorts, demonstrated that it's never too late to change. Never too late to be honest with yourself.

Whitely's fame was brief. While some of her coauthors went on another book tour, she went back to the deli. But she's grateful for all that has happened; for her new life with her boyfriend and her pet bird, Winston; for the support of her real-life sisters and her prison sisters; and for the possibilities of her craft.

In a note in the book, she says, "Writing's hard, but I feel a strong compulsion to do it. I wish I felt that way about exercising."

EPILOGUE

Following a barrage of press coverage (including Steve Kroft's report on *60 Minutes*), the state relented. Writers were permitted to keep their advances, and the state dropped its demand for incarceration repayment. Inmate Barbara Parsons Lane, of Warren, who had been awarded $25,000 from the PEN American Center (in protest of the state's policy and in support of the memoir project) was paroled after serving seven years of a ten-year sentence for manslaughter.

Part Six

POLITICS AS UNUSUAL

Mr. Ganim's Neighborhood

It is the columnist's duty to get away from the computer screen and plop himself physically in the heart of the matter. In this case, I was looking for a concrete way to present Bridgeport's issues of political scandal and urban distress. Much had been written about the corruption charges against Mayor Joseph Ganim, but I wanted a more intimate view. This required hanging out in the heart of his neighborhood, a place where a cross section of the population gathered daily. (Originally published March 2003)

Harborview Market is very much the picture described to me by its devotees except that, from the array of the activity advertised inside, I expected it to be much larger. I was surprised, too, by the decor, an eclectic array of furniture that might be described as American Tag Sale.

Even at 7:30 A.M., I was late if I intended to catch the real character of this landmark. By then, owner Rick Torres had finished baking the morning's croissants, and Andy Pantalone, one of the unofficial chefs, was already stuffing the cabbages to be sold later in the day. Dozens of patrons had filled cups from the selection of gourmet coffees and then gone off to offices or studios.

Two retired men in a corner booth were deep into their chess game, a king about to be cornered. One of the contestants, Wayne Hiller, would soon take his accustomed (and volunteer) position at the spinet to noodle a medley of jazz standards. The other, arts activist and concert performer Joseph Celli, was eager to drum up support for his new arts center (and then to lead me on a tour of the neighborhood in his green Jaguar).

Two women sitting near the makeshift stage (where many concerts have been held) had already reviewed the particulars of the *Connecticut Post* front page; it included yet another account from the political-corruption scandal that had become the trial of Bridgeport mayor Joe Ganim.

Ganim, who lives on Sailors Lane, a two-minute drive from the market in the upscale part of Black Rock, used to be a regular here. Owner Torres always made a huge fuss, announcing, "The mayor's in the house!"

This was during Ganim's political ascendancy—when *Newsweek* magazine ranked the articulate Democrat one of the twenty-five most influential mayors in the country. Ganim's vision for down-and-out Bridgeport was so inspiring that he seemed destined for the Governor's Residence in Hartford. This, of course, was well before the trouble was discovered—before what the *Connecticut Law Tribune* ranked as the biggest political corruption case in state history. Ganim found himself facing twenty-four federal counts, accused of benefiting from a wide array of kickback schemes that, in all, may have involved more than $1 million of illegal payoffs on projects that were worth hundreds of millions.

The trial, which began in January 2003, seemed likely to go on for months and would offer surprising twists. But one thing could be counted on: Ganim wouldn't be at the Harborview Market anytime soon. For all of the warmth of the place, there was no great desire to see Hizzoner, even though, it should be reported here, he ran up tabs that he always paid promptly.

The market seemed to be doing fine without him. On the morning of my visit, I talked to many customers who were willing to detail the virtues of the place and to reflect on the troublesome days ahead, not for Ganim, but for the Black Rock neighborhood.

I listened to their stories as piano man Hiller offered "Stardust," "This Can't Be Love," "The Surrey with the Fringe on Top," and, eerily, "Between the Devil and the Deep Blue Sea."

Don and Maxine Greenberg stopped at my table. He has been a political science professor at Fairfield University for more than three decades, and in 1998 he and Maxine (a clinical social worker) joined the Fairfield migration—perhaps twenty professors—to Black Rock. Greenberg, who teaches a course called Immigrant Politics among others, was eager to offer an academic explanation of Bridgeport's collapse. "The city has had poor leadership for some time. The infrastructure collapsed, schools deteriorated. Ethnic groups didn't get along with each other, intensifying the difficulties. It was impossible to attract middle-class students to the schools. Businesses and industries moved out. GE, Sikorsky, Bridgeport Brass. The city had a reputation for bad management, strong corruption, high taxes, little support form the state—adding up to a dismal picture." Greenberg recalled the hope that accompanied Ganim's rise. "He had some vision. And we got Harbor Yard [the ballpark], and downtown was being revitalized." But when hope is high, betrayal can be devastating.

This betrayal has turned the political tables. It is possible, although not all that probable, that in the future when someone at the Harborview says, "The mayor's in the house," he will be referring not to Ganim but to Rick Torres—the market's owner, a crois-sant baker, and a candidate for City Hall.

At forty-three years old, and with limited political experience (he ran for the school board and directed someone else's successful political campaign), Torres is running for mayor "out of necessity." And pragmatism. Though he has always been a Democrat, he is the Republican candidate. He thinks he can get on the ballot this way; otherwise, he'd be shut out by the Democratic machine. He is compelled to run, he says, out of self-preservation.

The erosion of the industrial and commercial tax base has left the city's financial burden on home owners. The result of all this is that while city services have dwindled, property taxes have doubled and even tripled. The Torres family, which includes five children, lives in a three-bedroom colonial and pays about $12,500 a year in taxes—more than someone who owns a million-dollar house in Cos Cob would pay. As a consequence of the tax burden, retired families who assumed they'd live in Black Rock forever have had to flee, as have young families who can't pay both exorbitant real estate taxes and tuition to private school for the kids (sending them to public school is unthinkable).

Still, Torres says, he and his wife, Michele (who works at Har-borview), intend to stay. "In a way, living here is stupid. It's a ques-tion of sanity. But I belong here. I grew up on these streets. I drank the hot chocolate and the lemonade that the neighbors gave me. This is where I fit."

Torres knows that he is a long shot as a candidate. Democrats are the force, and always have been the force, in Bridgeport. Tor-res needs a huge voter turnout to have a chance. But like any good candidate, he has confidence in his eyes, a strong platform of bet-ter schools and lower taxes, and a corruption-free program to lure industry. He argues that there is a clear chance for Bridgeport's resurrection.

Joseph Celli, who has lived in Hartford, New York City, and Miami, calls Bridgeport "a tough town" but hopes to contribute to the resurrection by demonstrating the power of art to lift the community spirit and economic base. He has brought world-class performers to town. Lincoln Center one night, Harborview Market the next. His new Black Rock Art Center will be a force—assuming all the money can be found to complete it. Celli, then, carries on the spirit of P. T. Barnum.

Barnum's life and work are instructive in this regard. He came back from devastating fires (one destroyed his home, "Iranistan," in Bridgeport, and another claimed two of his museums in New York). After the death of the primary attraction of his new circus—Jumbo, the elephant—everyone thought that the circus was dead. Until Barnum got the idea of putting Jumbo's bones on display. This made him another fortune. There is always a way, Bridgeport's most famous citizen showed, to climb out of the depths.

EPILOGUE

Joe Ganim was sentenced to nine years in federal prison. Rick Torres, as expected, lost to John M. Fabrizi, who was sworn in as Bridgeport's fifty-first mayor in April 2003. The city still faces large issues of taxes and revenues. Torres is part of a group that has put forward a billion-dollar redevelopment plan, "Gateway to a New Downtown," modeled after riverfront projects in San Antonio, Texas, and Providence, Rhode Island.

The Curry Touch

The Boys on the Bus is a classic book about political campaigning. It provides a view that's available only to those to see the process as it happens. When Bill Curry ran for governor in 2002 against John G. Rowland (a campaign that ultimately failed), I wanted to write The Boys in the Limo. *That never happened—Curry was too tightly scheduled. But when he saw that I wasn't going away, I was granted some access and was able to follow the candidate as he campaigned in Fairfield County, buoyed by improved poll results (which proved, in the end, to be misleading). (Originally published November 2002)*

Six weeks before the gubernatorial election, I waited outside Redding's Mark Twain Library for the chance to ask candidate Bill Curry one last question at the end of a long day on the campaign trail. The candidate, however, was occupied by a local reporter. At least six times the reporter earnestly demanded, "One last question, Mr. Curry." I was tempted to interrupt. "Young man, it is a rule in journalism—you may ask 'one last question' only three times, not six." But the working press is the working press. And in the season of elections, candidates adore the sound of their own voices.

In response to the peppering, Curry defended his tax reform plan, professed astonishment at Governor Rowland's about-face on casinos, and offered commentary on the significant issue of the night in Redding—Northeast Utilities' proposed new high-power line from Bethel to Norwalk. Curry opposes the new line, as do most of the people who attended the Communities For Responsible Energy meeting, which was still going on inside the building.

The reporter's grilling was finally cut off when a familiar face (and blonde hairstyle) appeared. Mary Travers, in a red shawl and black slacks, approached gingerly, with the aid of a cane. Earlier that night, the Mary of Peter, Paul, and Mary had held a private conversation with Curry during which he'd said to her, "I'm a big fan. I know all of your songs. But I won't inflict them on you tonight."

A few minutes later, Travers wanted to add a few points to the dialogue. She loves Redding, the town where she's lived since 1966, though in her view it is home to "too many Republicans." The singer told a story about putting out a green and white flag many years ago—before there was a widespread environmental movement—and being hauled before the local authorities, who accused her of being some kind of radical, which of course she was.

On this night, the candidate for governor and the aging folk singer exchanged business cards, and she went off in a blue Volvo. Finally, I asked Curry my one last question: "I've noticed your gift for humor. How do you think that humor can play a role in your campaign?" He thought a moment—the inquiry, after all, had strayed from the beaten path. Then he said, "I value my humor more than I do my eyesight."

This was something of a revelation, given the hostile tenor of the gubernatorial campaign. A woman I know, an immigrant from Peru, is among the most informed of ordinary citizens on matters of politics and public policy. When I told her about the time I spent with Curry, she said, "I didn't know that he is funny."

Perhaps I should amend this point. He is not the stand-up comic you would pay $75 a ticket to catch at Mohegan Sun. But if you had written a check for $50 to attend a fund-raising reception prior to the library meeting at the home of Redding supporters, you would have come away with the notion that Curry ranks, on the hilarity scale, well above Bill O'Neill, Lowell Weicker, and even the glib John Rowland.

Redding is an ideal spot for such a revelation. It has always been something of a center of humor. Josh Billings, a noted satirist, grew up there. Billings was big in his day (the late 1700s)—but not nearly as big, of course, as Mark Twain, who, as Sam Clemens, lived out the last eighteen months of his life in Redding (he died there in 1910), and whose largesse helped create the town's original public library.

Curry admires Twain's work. But if the candidate hoped to build bridges, he had to avoid Twain's particular brand of political humor. It was Twain, after all, who observed about our state capital, "I think I can say, and say with pride, that we have legislatures that bring higher prices than any in the world."

That's the problem. To be a humorist is to tell the truth. And to get into office as a politician, the truth must be painted, which is not at all the same thing. Bismarck, the nineteenth-century German chancellor, put it bluntly: "There are never more lies than after the hunt, before the wedding and before the election."

What you say, of course, depends on to whom you say it. At the fund-raising event in Redding, Curry was entirely among friends—out on the deck of a swell house with people who'd contributed to his underfinanced campaign. (At that point he trailed Rowland by only nine percentage points in the polls, a remarkable fact considering that he had been outspent six to one.) He could shoot from the hip, the way a much younger "Billy" Curry shot a basketball—from any point on the court and at any time.

Curry quoted a newspaper interview with Rowland. The governor had predicted that if Curry were elected, he'd sit around "intellectualizing" about global warming while our cities deteriorated. Curry pointed out that "a little intellectualizing never killed anyone" and that, in any case, "it's a condition from which one can recover." Standing near the ground on which new power lines would be built, Curry said, "John Rowland raises a fortune from the utilities. Of course, it doesn't necessarily go against his convictions to do so. The governor is not unduly encumbered by convictions."

Curry mixed his amusement with righteous indignation. He did not joke about global warming. He argued that people in Norwalk shouldn't have to put on sunblock in February. In this regard, he saw Rowland as the equivalent of Nero—citizens burning from ultraviolet rays as the governor fiddled, and not all that tunefully, either.

Curry must have been reminded on that evening—perhaps on every night as summer turned to fall—of his old Hartford neighborhood, where his parents were significant players in Democratic

Party politics. Curry's sister Kathleen (who worked full time in his campaign, along with several other family members) reported that the first word out of the mouths of all five children of Bill Sr. and Beverly was "vote."

It was a time of more passionate fighting for the underdog. Those were days when Catholics (like the Currys) lived with strict limitations. The Hartford insurance companies, for example, were notoriously anti-Catholic in their hiring and promotion policies. It was a time when Democratic causes, aligned so clearly with the underclasses, were vividly defined. That all changed. As Curry said, "Money overwhelms the democracy. Both parties are mortgaged to that interest."

He lamented the loss of interest in local politics. "As a child, I remember walking down Walnut Street with my father. We saw Dominic DeLucco, the mayor. He dressed like a mayor and held himself like a mayor. And he told my father, on the basis of very little evidence, that I was 'a fine young boy.' I thought, 'Gee, I've just met the mayor of Hartford.' Now, I meet parents who instruct their children to be excited when they meet 'the next governor.' But the children can't seem to do it."

Among adults there is cynicism, and there is indifference. There is also, in many places, the presumption that politics is a game entirely for insiders. About his candidacy for governor in its earliest stages, Curry told me, "In my own family, I'm not sure I had a majority of the Currys who thought I had a chance."

But they became believers (even as they fretted over steady slippage in the polls that September). They saw in him more determination and more fire than when he first challenged Rowland in 1994. He saw himself, in his early fifties, as more mature, more able to influence. But he also used his sense of humor to disarm and to charm. Connecticut voters got to see this quality in a series of October debates held with the governor. Back then, Curry still had enough time to argue, with the help of a few clever phrases, that reports of the death of his candidacy were mildly exaggerated.

Field Tripping

News reporters swarmed over the state capitol when the legislature undertook hearings to determine whether to impeach then-governor John G. Rowland. My deadline for Connecticut *magazine, and the lag time required for printing, dictated that my technique in coverage had to be different than those who were working for daily newspapers or television. I needed to write something that would stand the test of time, no matter what the legislature decided to do. So instead of covering the hearings, I went downstairs and was lucky enough to stumble on a tour being given to elementary students from Groton. I knew that this would be my focus—the juxtaposition of innocence and, upstairs in the lofty chambers, great cynicism. This is a strong example of the necessity of a writer's "being there," as opposed to hearing stories secondhand or simply doing interviews. (Originally published August 2004)*

Teachers arrange field trips months in advance. So there was no way to foresee that third graders from S. B. Butler Elementary in Groton would tour the State Capitol on precisely the wrong day.

Or, depending on the point of view, precisely the right day.

In the hour before these children arrived in Hartford on June 8, television trucks turned a Capitol parking lot into an electronics display. A newspaper photographer waited (in vain, it turned out) to get a picture of the besieged governor. Upstairs, in the Old Judiciary Room, legislators assembled to consider the weighty question of impeachment.

The process was, from the start, slow and cumbersome, and it left reporters scrambling for something dramatic to record in their notebooks. During the break on that first afternoon, six TV cameramen focused on the men's room exit, hoping to get footage more significant than lawyers zipping their flies.

Then into this historic building came the third graders from Groton. They had eager faces and names like Jocelyn, Christina, Eden, Max, Gage, Zachary, Annika, and Ashley. For almost all of them, it was their first glimpse of the halls of government.

The tour guide greeted them near the entrance. She said, "Today we have to be extra quiet. Something very important is happening up on the third floor." This didn't seem to register. Instead the children stared at the eye-popping features in a spectacular building finished in 1878, a creamy version of Oz.

The children had been prepared well. None of them was stumped by the statue of the Official State Hero. Nathan Hale was on the lips of everyone. "He was so young when he passed away," said Eden. Yes, passed away. As in hanged for what the British considered treasonous spying and what Revolutionaries considered selfless patriotism. That's the trouble. How to teach the children myth from reality. How to make sense of a heritage steeped in stained glass, Italian marble, and human riddles.

And yet, out of the mouths of babes come new riddles. One of the third graders asked the guide, "Do we breathe in the molecules of the people of a long time ago?" The guide, clearly stumped, responded, "That might be a good question for your classroom." A demonstration of the art, so well developed in this historic place, of buck passing.

In the next hour, the children visited the empty chambers of the legislature. The guide asked them, "After a bill passes the House and Senate, who signs it?"

A boy raised his hand and answered, "George W. Bush." The guide corrected him. "It's our state's governor, John G. Rowland. And what's it called if the governor won't sign it?" A boy answered, "A veto." She then asked how many votes it takes for the legislature to override a veto—"the answer is a fraction." The boy responded, "One half and a quarter left of it." Though not accurate, perhaps close enough for government work.

State Senator Catherine W. Cook, who attended S. B. Butler as a child, met the children in the Senate chambers. She tailored her remarks for third-grade ears, but it was rough going at first. As she recounted her typical legislative day—starting with a 6:00 A.M. breakfast meeting and ending seventeen hours later—her audience seemed indifferent. Hey, kids have long days, too, engaged in the hard work of childhood. So they rubbed their hands on the plush carpet, elbowed each other, and used every reliable body motion to get through the lesson.

Sensing their restlessness, Cook told the kids that she had supported a successful bill that required every school to have recess. The children roared their approval. Then Senator Cook pointed to the state motto, emblazoned on the carpeting. "Does anyone know what *Qui Transtulit Sustinet* means?" A girl answered, "It means when you come from one place to another, you keep going." A boy offered, "It means the Lord sent us here and still watches over us."

The children, it turned out, were spared watching over the third floor. There would be no visit on this day to the governor's office or the Old Judiciary Room. And Senator Cook, who is a Republican, had no real interest in talking much about the hearings. But if she had, she might have told the children a story:

"Once, boys and girls, a young man not all that much older than you was elected by citizens of his district to represent them in this beautiful place. He was impressed, as you were, by the statue of Nathan Hale. And by the golden dome. But, of course, the golden dome is deceiving. The gold is only three one-hundredths of an inch thick. Things in this building, and in life, are often not what they appear on the surface.

"When you are in a position of power, as this young man was, you make friends. The problem is, you don't really know if they become your friends because they like you or because you can do something for them. But if you are ambitious, as our young hero was, you may not take the time to figure out the difference, and, besides, you need all the help you can get.

"Just a few years later the people of our state elected the young man to Congress in Washington. He served three terms in the House of Representatives and then came home, where he campaigned for governor. He was only thirty-seven years old. That sounds ancient to you, but believe me, it isn't. In fact, he became the youngest person ever to sit in the Connecticut governor's chair. And one of the most passionate. He set out to help our cities.

He raised a lot of money for UConn, supported the arts, and worked to bring new industry here. He also knew how to comfort people in times of tragedy—he visited the families that lost relatives in the attack on the World Trade Center.

"He loved being governor, and it showed. Old people and young were impressed. But he never did learn the difference between real friends and people who would take advantage of him.

"You see, boys and girls, no one is all good or all bad—not even Nathan Hale or John G. Rowland. Everybody has flaws. Sometimes people can overcome their flaws. But in the case of this governor, this was not so. He had many big bills to pay and was not a rich man. And so he told himself, what would it hurt if some of his so-called friends bought him things for his house, or sent him on vacations? It didn't matter if these friends also did business with the state, and their favors might appear to help them get rich contracts. The governor had worked hard and done good things. He felt he had a right to live in the style in which his friends lived.

"But, of course, he knew in his heart, all along the way, that what he was doing was wrong. And he did nothing about it, except let it continue. That is why important meetings begin today upstairs—to determine if he should be removed from office because he used his position to enrich himself, which is something a public servant should never do.

"And so, when you look around here, you see a place where not only greatness has been achieved, but failure as well. You can think of this building as a lesson for you. Don't be too impressed by appearances. Always ask yourself if you're doing the right thing. No matter what anyone else tells you, you know the real answer."

That Senator Cook said none of this was not surprising. She looked out at Eden, Max, Gage, and the others and must have concluded that they would lose their innocence soon enough. Before the children were bused back to Groton, she invited each to sit in the historic Wishing Chair, made out of the trunk of the famous Charter Oak tree. She said, "This is where the lieutenant governor, Jodi Rell, sits when she presides over the Senate."

Senator Cook then whispered an aside to me, "She probably wishes that she can be the governor." In this historic place, because of the triumph of human frailties, and as a compelling lesson for impressionable youth, that wish has come to pass.

EPILOGUE

Before the legislature completed its inquiry, John G. Rowland resigned from office. Later a federal judge sentenced him to one year and one day in prison, followed by four months of house arrest.

Coming Home

When the United States invaded Iraq in 2003, the local news media kept track of a unit from Connecticut. When the unit returned, I noticed in the accounts of the homecoming a Vietnamese name. The father of a soldier was quoted perfunctorily. It occurred to me that there was a chance that I could find the elusive connection between the wars in Vietnam and Iraq. (Originally published November 2004)

On the day that his oldest son would return home from Iraq, Hoang Dinh excused himself from the second shift at Colt Firearms in West Hartford and drove his Honda Accord to a gym in New Haven. Someone else at the plant would have to manufacture the tools used to make M16 rifles. Dinh would be otherwise occupied, waiting and worrying. Which is what he had done so often in his life.

Dinh took his seat in the bleachers. Around him were other relatives of the members of the 439th Quartermaster Company, scheduled to arrive by bus at 6:00 P.M. Most of the soldiers were represented by family hordes, but Dinh sat alone. His wife was at work at the beautician shop not far from their house in East Hartford. His younger son was in class at UConn.

That the buses were late did not surprise Dinh. This was the same bureaucratic U.S. Army that he came to know long ago, when it spent a decade and a half in Vietnam, his native country.

As he sat and waited for the company of returnees, he understood the irony of the circumstance. Dinh, a man of considerable intellect who attended law school back home, knew that in some sense he sat not only in a bleacher in New Haven but at the intersection of Baghdad and Saigon.

Much has been made of the correlation between two infamous wars, particularly as the presidential election season intensified. Hoang Dinh and his family make that connection personally. He was more than a witness to America's disastrous and divisive attempt to aid South Vietnam. He fought in that war, survived it, and in its aftermath risked everything he had. But when he finally made it to this country, Dinh discovered that he, too, would have to send a son off to a war born of deceit, a war that could ultimately prove unsupportable.

Dinh received many letters from Iraq during his son Lance's nearly eighteen-month tour with the 439th. He could see that Lance was a good soldier who quietly did his duty and offered a steady hand in refueling efforts in the desert—qualities that earned him a promotion to specialist.

But even a bright young man who'd earned an electrical engineering degree from Trinity College couldn't explain the meaning of this war to his father or to himself. In his contact with ordinary Iraqis, Lance saw desperation. Among these people, there was no talk of freedom or democracy. It was merely a struggle for everyday survival, the nasty and demeaning circumstance of real war. Not the "Washington speak" of artful dodgers who once specialized in deferments or special treatment and who have since refashioned themselves as blind hawks who consider any opposition un-American.

Though clearly loyal and competent at his work, Lance didn't have a perfect record. He got busted from specialist to private first class for doing what we all did every night back in Vietnam—that is, drink a beer or two. Alcohol is banned in today's war. Though his was a minor sin, Lance knew better and considered his actions "stupid."

He grew up knowing the rules and taking nothing for granted. Lance witnessed the obstacles and courage it took merely to survive in a dangerous world.

His father lived a life of sacrifice. It was a far cry from what Hoang Dinh imagined for himself as a young man in Saigon, addicted as he was to Bridget Bardot and Claudia Cardinale movies. In fact, Lance's parents tell a love story interrupted so often and so dramatically that it must have baffled their sons as to how they ever got together.

It was 1974 when Hoang Dinh and Ut Be Vo met, began dating, and fell in love. But Dinh went off as a lieutenant in the Army of the Republic of Vietnam, fighting Ho Chi Minh's army from the north and the insurgent Viet Cong from the south. When the war finally ended on April 30, 1975, the new government sent Dinh to a prison camp, where he spent twenty-eight months and was grilled for information. He could see that the government was in chaos, unfamiliar with the territory and personalities, or the divisions within it—a precursor to what his son would eventually find in Iraq. Dinh wrote letters to his wife, letters that were read first by highly suspicious government officials.

After his release, Hoang Dinh and Ut Be Vo were married. But even then, separation was inevitable. As a former enemy officer,

Dinh was not allowed in the cities and was sent off to plant and harvest rice, tasks for which he had no aptitude. Meanwhile, Vo lived in Can Tho. Eventually, Dinh was allowed into the city. That's where the family began to plot an escape.

But they had enough gold saved—twenty ounces—to buy only two passages on a secret vessel. Dinh's wife and youngest son, Hung, would have to stay behind. And so in 1984, Dinh and five-year-old Lance were among the 170 passengers on a 40-foot boat that left the Mekong Delta and headed toward Malaysia. Storms nearly overturned the vessel. Food ran out; there was nothing to eat for nearly three days. Finally, the engine died.

Years later, as an adult, Lance wondered how his father took care of a five-year-old who suffered terrible hunger pangs. "I must have cried and cried." It was only when the boat drifted toward an oil rig that the passengers were rescued. Even then, the escapees had to go to camps in the Philippines to learn English and to await sponsorship in America.

Hoang Dinh's sponsorship came from a man who had been a fellow political prisoner. The friend offered Dinh a job at a nursing home in Wethersfield. So began the effort to adjust to America, and to save enough money to buy enough gold so that a year later his wife and younger son could embark on a similar arduous journey to freedom.

In early August 2004, as Dinh waited in those New Haven bleachers for Lance to come home, he considered his position as just another American trying to support his government but not quite getting the full picture. Too complicated, he thought. Even so, he saw the invasion of Iraq as useful in the fight against terror. He wouldn't question the wisdom of invading and occupying. In all likelihood, he would never have had the chance to buy a house here, and to have a good job, if America hadn't made the mistake of waging war in Vietnam.

That's part of the legacy—a bevy of anecdotal human evidence about the value of fighting for freedom. I have a friend who runs a popular Asian restaurant in Rocky Hill who wouldn't be here otherwise. I know a brilliant new grad at Brown University (she scored a perfect 1,600 on her SATs) whose uncle was once the mayor of Hanoi; she wouldn't be here otherwise. Twenty years from now, there will be Iraqi-born American citizens who will similarly dazzle academic America the way she has. But the question is, are divisive war-mongering policies and huge sacrifices in lives and money the only way to get them here?

In New Haven, at about 8:50 P.M., the buses finally pulled in. The soldiers filed out of the doors and into one last formation. They endured earnest but long-winded speeches by their superiors and the words of Senator Christopher Dodd, who said, "Regardless of one's views of the politics of it all, all Americans, regardless of opinion, express their gratitude to you." If the senator had excised one "regardless" from his speech, the soldiers could have broken ranks a millisecond earlier to collect their hugs—as Lance Dinh finally did with his much-relieved father—and to begin the process of figuring out what eighteen months in the desert meant to their lives and to their country.

Lance is home now, in East Hartford, planning to use the GI bill for graduate study in industrial design. After twenty-five years of going where the political winds pointed, he wants at last to set off in his own direction.

Part Seven

THE BUSINESS
OF CONNECTICUT

A Case of Connecticut Wining

Here was a chance to address one of my favorite contin-
uing subjects: Connecticut's view of itself. In this case,
how seriously does it take its wine industry, and how
seriously should we as consumers take it? It helps, in
selling the piece to readers, if your vineyard owner is
the chairman of Tiffany & Co. (Originally published
January 1997)

In the matter of wine, a person never learns. She begins with a taste of something sweet, sacramental perhaps, and she graduates in young adulthood to what she thinks is more serious, something Riunite-like, or a pleasant rosé from Portugal. Then one day she attends a dinner party and learns that there's more to life than sugar. Friends begin to talk to her of bouquet and tannin and nose and of the curious matter of "breathing." Friends say, "There will be no more Lambrusco for you."

And so her education in French begins, and she becomes acquainted with various country chateaux. She experiments with other vintages from France, and from certain regions of Italy, and learns, of course, about the impressive fruits of California. She is confident that she now knows enough to thoroughly examine a wine list on behalf of important clients.

She sits, on this day, at the prestigious 21 Club in Manhattan and examines the selection of chardonnay. Oh yes, of course, here's Matanzas Creek, Kistler, Grgich Hills from California, and some recognizable French names. And here's—wait a minute, this must be a misprint—a wine from Connecticut, from a vineyard called Chamard in a town called Clinton. She is befuddled. She is reminded that just when a person thinks she knows what she is doing in this life, she discovers evidence to the contrary. She is reminded that the business of wineries and snobberies gets more confusing all the time. So she orders safely. She orders California.

What she doesn't know is what most people don't know, including most of the gentle residents of Connecticut, who, just as residents of every other province on earth, assume that whatever is local is, at best, second-rate. The people in Connecticut are convinced that other places have the real answers and we are mere pretenders.

In the matter of the art world, that supposition proves false. So it is in the matter of ingenuity and invention. And in the matter of wine, well, perhaps the case should not be overstated. California vintners, after all, have been around for a long time and have produced many wonderful wines. That state's large producers create more wine in a year than all of the vineyards in Connecticut combined. Connecticut wine is a new business, inaugurated in 1975 in Litchfield County by Sherman Haight, of Haight Vineyards, who also helped establish something very unusual: a loose federation of competitors who actually aided and encouraged each other, gave advice, and loaned equipment and commiserated when problems occurred. These entrepreneurs work apart and together. They understand that their welfare depends to a large degree on the growth and the promotion of one of the state's undervalued industries.

And so the folks at Haight Vineyards have nice things to say about the ethics and products of, say, Hopkins Vineyard in New Preston. Bill Hopkins, while pointing out the virtues of his own wines (which have won medals in national and international competition), is not shy about mentioning how he and the winemaker of Chamard talk all the time about new pruning techniques or advanced trellis systems. And Nick Smith of Stonington Vineyards—who in a blind tasting in Boston surprised a lot of Frenchmen who found their own wines ranked below his—is an enthusiastic promoter in the matter of the state's winemaking. "Local doesn't mean cheap. Local means good." Of Chamard, he offers many compliments. He talks of his great regard for the winemaker there. And says, "Of course, the [winemaker's] boss has not spared the finest equipment." After only a few years in the business, the boss is already locally legendary. He inspires Nick Smith at Stonington to remind us of the old saying that, "If you want to make a small fortune in the wine business, start out with a big fortune."

Bill Chaney, the sixty-four-year-old owner of Chamard, is chairman of Tiffany & Co., the very Manhattan establishment that attracted Truman Capote's fictional character Holly Golightly and every person who ever admired fine jewelry. This is the Tiffany of the blue box. This is the Tiffany that has gone way beyond Fifth Avenue to more than a hundred stores all over the world, an expansion that requires Chaney to do a good deal of traveling and a good deal of looking forward to his weekend retreat. He and his family have been coming to Clinton since the early 1970s because, he says, if he doesn't go there on weekends he is pretty hard to live with.

I met him on a Friday in the "chateau," the winemaking building that was designed exclusively for the property, the headquarters of a vineyard that produces about 6,000 cases a year. In his office, Chaney looked very Tiffanyish, although I can't say he wore any jewelry. Still, you know the silver-haired corporate look, and the easy corporate smile, and the crisp business shirt, and the deep voice that puts a positive spin on everything.

But it would be far too simple, and inaccurate, to say that Bill Chaney is merely the money guy. He bleeds this wine. He may look corporate to us now, but he was the one on his hands and knees building that marvelous (and very long) stone wall, what he calls "a three-dimensional jigsaw." And he (and his family and friends) were the ones in the early days, before the fancy equipment arrived, who helped harvest grapes. "There's nothing wrong with hard labor."

The family, by the way, would naturally have an interest. The very name Chamard does not refer to some French region but is a tribute to the Chaney children—Caroline, Matt, Carol, and Diana—with letters taken from their names and the family surname. "Chamard sounded like a proper wine," Chaney says.

A proper wine requires a great deal of emotional investment, a willingness to withstand the vexing problems of winemaking. No matter your money or your ability to find suitable land and a fine winemaker, there are the matters of hurricanes, weather variations, and birds. Bill Chaney remembers that a third of his very first crop was lost because in that dry summer, the finches, robins, and bluebirds had no place to find liquid refreshment except at the heart of his chardonnay grapes.

He and his winemaker, Larry McCulloch, tried everything. They hired teenagers to drive around the acreage in all-terrain vehicles to scare birds away. They tried noisemakers every few minutes that sounded like shotguns. "It was not very pleasant in the neighborhood." They tried, finally, the complicated and time-consuming business of netting. And now, all these years later, it is safe to say that more people and fewer birds have become aware of these grapes.

People have become aware of this because, Chaney says, of the special skills of the man who grows the grapes and makes the wine, who has a special feeling for what it takes to succeed. He lives in the other half of the chateau, looking out over the twenty acres, planning, scheming, worrying, tinkering, and spending perhaps more time out in the field than any winemaker in Connecticut.

There is another old expression in this business: "It takes a lot of beer to make a good wine." That is, it's hard, hot work, and the last thing a person in the field wants is a glass of wine. If that is truly the case, Larry McCulloch was perfectly suited for the job of winemaker. He grew up in Amish country in rural Ohio, a beer-drinking region. And his education as a winemaker was not really by design.

In his formative years, Larry had intentions of entering woodland management conservation. But after graduating from Ohio State, he could find no such positions in the want ads, and so he went where the opportunities were. He brought his beer (and Riunite) taste to the East, where New York vineyards were looking for educated hands, and got his introduction to winemaking over several years at Benmarl, a winery in the Hudson Valley.

In time, Larry was promoted to winemaker. "I didn't know anything about wine, but I did know how to hire a consultant." It turned out to be a crucial hire, because the consultant taught Larry about the chemistry of wine. He learned how to measure sugar, acidity levels, and alcohol and how to adjust these properties. He learned of yeast from Burgundy and of French oak for barrels. He learned the special qualities of grapes grown in the Northeast, where there is a great deal more moisture than in California but also a great deal more acidity. For that reason it made no sense to try to produce California-style wines. In climate and terrain, the East Coast resembles regions of Europe, whose vineyards became the models.

Larry developed a great passion for the business and soon made a name for himself, which brought him to the attention of the man with the money.

On the occasions when I visited Chamard, Larry seemed scarce. Visitors, after all, spend time in the tasting room. (Chamard, like most Connecticut vineyards, welcomes visitors, offers tastes, and sells its wines on the premises.) Larry is seldom in this room; in fact, when I bought a bottle of 1994 Estate Reserve Chardonnay, he didn't know where to stash the $12.99.

This end of the business is for others. His end is down in the basement in the bottling process, or in filling the oak barrels, or in checking the chemistry, or going outside where he loves it best, in the fields. In the winter he is trimming the vines, cutting off last year's growth, getting just the right balance, keeping enough new wood. In the spring he is controlling the weeds, replanting, fertilizing, checking for bud damage. In the summer he is making sure that the growing is on schedule and that the trellis system is working. In fall, of course, is the harvest and the bottling of the previous season's bounty.

At all times there is the struggle to improve the grape quality, to streamline techniques, to learn more, to squeeze a better bottle of wine out of the yield. And there is always the matter of the unexpected, as in one year during the fermentation process when that horrible smell we all remember from chemistry lab—rotten eggs—emerged. What to do? Was the year's work wasted? No. Hydrogen sulfide is a common problem in winemaking. The French, as a rule, don't mind if a little of the smell creeps into the bottle—it adds to the "complexities." All the same, Larry McCulloch would rather not sell such complex wine; there's already enough vinegar sold in the world. He learned how to break down the gas. And, like all winemakers who face crises (which is every winemaker), he thought positively.

It all came out all right, of course. But even Larry was surprised at the results of a very public event that challenged his and Chamard's candidacy as one of the up-and-coming names in the business.

In 1993 *Cook's Illustrated* magazine sponsored a blind tasting and invited Larry to be one of the judges. "I wouldn't have done it if I had known my wine was going to be among those tasted," he said. The potential for embarrassment was high; no winemaker wants to suffer the humiliation of being on hand when low scores are issued or, worse, having judged all of the wines presented anonymously in brown paper bags, of giving a low score to his own product.

That night, there was no convivial conversation—no talking at all, just the tasting, sniffing, and swishing around of fourteen white chablis-style wines, European and American, including Chamard's 1990 Estate Reserve. The judges rated each glass on a scale of one through seven.

"I thought I could find mine," Larry recalls, "but I couldn't put my finger on it. I was sweating bullets."

When it was over, the other judges wanted to see what Larry had done to his own wine, to see if he had destroyed it. They grabbed his notes. But, no, he hadn't destroyed it. He had rated his wine highly, and so, it turned out, had everyone else. In fact, the judges ranked it much more highly than a French wine that sold for more than $50 a bottle. Of the fourteen competitors, the Chamard finished second with thirty-six points, losing out by a mere two points to a $40 bottle of French wine, 1990 Fevre Grand Cru "Les Clos." Here is the *Cook's Illustrated* account of what the judges said about the Chamard: "From a fledgling vineyard by the Long Island Sound, this wine demonstrates that the East Coast holds great promise for the future of Chardonnay in the United States. Most tasters found it a bit austere but extremely well made."

Larry McCulloch's reaction: "We are now more brave and confident about ourselves."

So this is a success story, but only the beginnings of one. There is much to be done: better wine yet to be made and, surely, a better way to get the word out about another of Connecticut's valuable industries. For the fact is that Chamard wouldn't appear on the wine list of the prestigious 21 Club if not for the influence of the man who runs Tiffany, the man who, according to the club's beverage director, is the only customer to order it.

China Syndrome

My intent here was to demonstrate how the world economy and competition factors affect Connecticut jobs. It is one thing to read about statistics that show the growth of Asian manufacturing and its impact on American employment, and it's quite another to show that impact in human terms, which is, of course, the way that I prefer. I didn't anticipate having the chance to speak to a worker whose life story would provide rich perspective. But I should have known—when you hang around, you always find a miracle. (Originally published December 2003)

Somewhere in China, there is a plot afoot to oust New Britain factory workers from their jobs. The tactics are shameless—a case of international counterfeiting. But I should begin this tale of industrial intrigue where former governor John G. Rowland learned of it and where it became, for him, something of an obsession.

Early in the summer of 2003, the governor attended a meeting of the Council of Economic Development and Technology at the Webster Bank boardroom in Waterbury. One of the room's walls is covered by a large mural depicting the Brass City's downtown in its heyday. This setting, then, was suitable for a discussion about deterioration. The group addressed the debilitating numbers—26,000 manufacturing jobs lost in our state since 2001.

During the discussion, Matt Guyer, president of Reflexite Americas in New Britain, sat quietly for nearly two hours, awaiting his turn. He listened to others as they offered an accounting of manufacturing impediments in Connecticut—health-care costs, high wages, and, of course, competition from cheap labor in the Third World. The usual China bashing. But when it came Guyer's moment to talk, the governor became aware of the new problem from Asia.

Guyer described his product stock. Reflexite Americas is part of Reflexite Corporation (world headquarters in Avon), which produces materials that require a distinct technology language: "conspicuity" and "retroflective" and "microprism design." There are—you can count them, should you have the eyesight and the tools to do it—at least 47,000 microprisms per square inch in what Reflexite makes: the safety material that glows in the dark on firefighter outfits, eighteen-wheelers, construction cones on the highway, and school buses, among many other uses.

The company has produced this product locally for decades, since the founders, brothers Bill and Hugh Rowland (no relationship to any prominent politician), first had the notion that microprism technology in Connecticut could compete favorably with 3M. The Minnesota corporate giant used glass beads for its reflective materials. The difference was that Reflexite produced a more intense reflection and therefore a product that had more value.

Competing with 3M was one thing, but Matt Guyer wasn't in Waterbury to tell the instructive story about how Reflexite won the coveted John Deere account over its chief domestic rival by precisely matching the company's intense shade of yellow. He was there to tell the governor about the threat to Connecticut jobs not by honest competition, but by outright thievery.

John Rowland told Guyer's story of "the smoking gun" to all New England governors and to the Advisory Committee for Trade Policy and Negotiations, in Washington, D.C. He showed all these people the evidence of industrial theft: two lime green patches of reflective vinyl. One of them was produced by workers at the Reflexite Americas plant in New Britain and stamped with the Reflexite logo; the other was produced by workers in an unknown location in China and also stamped with the Reflexite logo, to make it look authentic. With the naked eye it is impossible to tell the vinyl specimens apart. It is also impossible to discern that the Reflexite business cards and product literature produced in China are phony, too.

In a world where knockoffs of clothing, watches, and other goods have become routine, there is a new and horrifying development: technology knockoffs that have large safety consequences. Brake pads. Prescription medicine. And now, conspicuity (the property of being visually conspicuous). Altogether, it's an international problem with financial consequences in the billions. Locally, Matt Guyer estimates that knockoffs cost Reflexite about 4 percent of its gross income and hurt its reputation because, he says, "these products are not as good." They don't last. They don't have the sophisticated microprism technology—just the ability to make them look like a Connecticut product.

What's happening in China is a violation of international law, but, as of yet, the perpetrators are still at work. The federal government, from all indications, will press China to investigate. Meanwhile, it is business as usual, and unusual, in New Britain.

I spent a day at the Reflexite Americas factory, an airy place decorated with plants and family photos at work stations. That's where I met forty-seven-year-old Emilia Podkoviak. Her story reflects, if that word is not overused here, a remarkable corporate strategy that made the company, according to the Connecticut Psychological Association, one of the five in the state designated a psychologically healthy workplace in 2002. (The others were FleetBoston Financial, American Eagle Federal Credit Union, Gaylord Hospital, and Wheeler Clinic.)

Emilia arrived in this country in 1983 from her native Poland. Her husband was here already, having landed factory work in New Britain. Though Emilia had earned a college degree in her homeland, she found no work at first, not even house cleaning. Language was a big issue. When a neighbor brought her to Reflexite and Emilia landed an entry-level job in the plant, she still knew only a few words of English: "good," "no good," "hi," "bye," and, most important, "help!"

Orders would come down from the boss—in those days, Reflexite had a typical industrial setup—and someone would translate for her. New Britain has many Polish immigrants, all of whom had to learn English at their own speed. Many of them took industrial jobs for companies that, in the end, did not show the kind of loyalty to the city that Reflexite has.

When the founders of the business retired, they could have sold out to 3M. Instead, the Rowland brothers created an employee-owned company, guaranteeing that local jobs would be saved. As Bill Rowland explained it to me in a phone interview, his father had been chief chemist at Stanley Works during the Depression and worked hard to save jobs—this would be the Rowland family legacy. So each Reflexite worker, no matter the level, would earn shares of stocks, dividends, and monthly bonuses based on company earnings.

"My first monthly bonus," Emilia recalls, "was one dollar or two dollars. But anyway, it was something." As business built, particularly when the federal government ordered that all eighteen-wheelers on the road had to have reflective material along the sides and back, it was a boon to employees. There were months when some employees earned bonuses as high as $500. Before regularly scheduled meetings in which Matt Guyer goes over the finances with everyone—from accountants to people who sweep the floors—Emilia already knows the substance of his message because she gauges how much work there has been in the factory.

This, indeed, is a rare business. And Emilia and her colleagues feel much more a part of it. Now there are seven teams, and Emilia is one of the team leaders.

I watched these teams as they performed the work and was struck by the intensity of it and the obvious commitment. The teams work at each task (at machines that cut, or where the finished plastic must be separated) with great attention to detail and an eye for eliminating waste—as if their own livelihood depended on their own nimble hands, because to a large degree it does.

For Emilia, who began her working life in Poland in a socialist society where people simply did what they were told, this is all a revelation. And yet she sees the irony that workers in China, probably laboring as she once did in her country in insufferable conditions, are now endangering her livelihood here.

She knows the details of the threat as well as anyone. But like Matt Guyer, she also has a sense of confidence. There are some reasons for optimism. The government is about to introduce a new highway color—in the conspicuity industry this is huge news. Coral will indicate "crash ahead." Mostly, there is confidence that, in the end, Connecticut quality will win out and the industrial thieves will be caught. If not, Reflexite's own plant in China may knock off the knockoffs.

And yet Emilia is also realistic. She knows that legitimate competition from the Third World will endanger the business of highway-cone reflectors and other product lines. She is aware that one day Reflexite could simply exist as just another exhibit at the nearby New Britain Industrial Museum.

"We're still keeping those jobs," she told me. "But who knows? They won't stay forever. We need to make what we're making in a shorter time. As for the future: Let's hope."

Part Eight

PERSONALLY SPEAKING

Sixty Rules

Writers I know have commented on the trap of personal pieces. Readers love them, but these pieces can be cloying and gratuitous, not to mention gallingly self-referential. It is necessary to offer a wider perspective so that the writer is not saying to the reader, "Gee, isn't my life fascinating?" Instead, even while necessarily relating extensive detail, he or she is saying, "Here's my life in as broad a context as I can relate it." Also, the only worthwhile personal writing leaves a little of the writer's skin on the sidewalk. (Originally published January 2004)

An issue of the AARP magazine arrived at the house in timely fashion, with an optimistic cover message: "Sixty is the New Thirty." And then, at the grocery store, I couldn't help but notice the discovery of an "anti-aging" pill announced boldly on the cover of *Reader's Digest.*

Oh what a joyous era to be, as my late dear friend Leonora Hays used to say, "old and decapitated."

A woman I know argued that for a columnist, a sixtieth birthday is too juicy a subject to pass up. I argued that, indeed, it can be passed up and ought to be passed up. Most columnists who foist their milestone birthdays on readers send whiny or self-aggrandizing messages that barely scratch the wrinkling and tender surface of aging or reflect its genuine traumas and fears.

Mark Twain addressed the subject stylishly, of course. "Life would be infinitely happier if we could only be born at the age of 80 and gradually approach 18." He also wrote, "When I was younger I could remember anything, whether it happened or not; but I am getting old, and soon I shall remember only the latter."

This is how the elegant writer Bice Clemow, of West Hartford, documented the mind's decline in an essay he wrote for *Northeast:* "I can forget that I just brushed my teeth, yet remember, hardly without thinking, the name of the nice woman who clerked in Wm. Power's men's store twenty years ago . . . Young friends of mine (that's people sixty) complain about forgetting names, addresses, and recipes, a confession presumed to make us dodders feel better about the degenerative generation. Whoever called it the Golden Age wasn't in it. Better would be the Daze of the Open Fly."

At sixty (the actual birthday was November 13, 2004), I am not yet in the Golden Age, although on more than one occasion a dear and caring friend has pointed out before I was about to appear in public that I really ought to have a daily, or perhaps hourly, zipper check.

But sixty as thirty? On the face of it, absurd, a ploy simply to call attention to AARP's blind advocacy. At thirty I was not yet reliant on the pharmaceutical industry to address depression, blood pressure, cholesterol, thyroid problems, or, to refer to the condition tastefully, erectile issues.

At thirty I was a babe, even though I knew death's sting. Yes, like so many others, I'd watched grandparents wither and die. But I also saw death in ways that others hadn't—first in Vietnam. And then at home. On the verge of my thirtieth birthday, my first wife died of an aneurysm. I tried to become both the mother and father to our three-year-old daughter, Amy—a task that, frankly, overwhelmed me.

I had thought in Vietnam, before all this, that all I had to do was survive the slings and arrows and land mines and poisoned sticks of the VC, and life as I knew it would go on forever.

Tell this to my periodontist, who has pulled four of my teeth and promises to pull more if I don't prove better at "home care." Tell it to my internist, who warns me that sleeping pills are understandably useful but potentially addictive. Tell it to my therapist, who suggested part of my anxiety might be that Big Birthday.

On the other hand, I have had many inspiring role models in the matter of aging, beginning with the natural one, my mother. She survived quite nicely in the years after my father's death, and at age eighty-four, was still touring in the condominium's Kazoo Band (she was the third from the right in the second row), playing concerts for those she called "the old people." When she died, she did so efficiently and without inordinate pain—a life lived 99.7 percent in good health and with vigor.

I think, too, of Laurent de Brunhoff, who has a house in Middletown. There he works on his Babar books. These are ageless—the adventures of a young elephant as drawn by a man approaching eighty who has the body of an Olympic sprinter, and whose daily yoga regimen is strenuous and, at the same time, elegant.

I think of the woman I called the Lady in White, Florence Berkman. She was the art critic for the old *Hartford Times* and the wife of political columnist Moses Berkman. Often, when spring-time got warm enough, I visited Florence's home, which was the carriage house for the Governor's Residence, and we'd have lunch in the backyard. She always had strong opinions about Connecti-cut first ladies and ranted about how some of them were indiffer-ent to style, taste, and history.

In her nineties, Florence remained gorgeous—white hair care-fully groomed, a wardrobe exclusively pale to set off her rich skin color, her bright eyes reflecting a nonstop thought process. She wrote every day on an old Royal typewriter, manufactured in her city many decades before, still using carbon paper. She wrote awk-wardly and never had any use for subtlety, but she had something to say and was always engaged in saying it.

When I visited in the spring of her eighty-ninth year, Florence had been told that she had cancer. I said I was sorry and asked how she was handling it and what had to be done. She responded, "Oh, I don't know. Cancer's not my problem. It's the doctor's problem." Florence lived a decade longer, until the age of ninety-nine.

That was the age at which Helaine Gorski, the waitress at the Dannheiser Inn in Berlin, died. She had worked until two years before, waiting on tables and running the place with her niece, Hildegard Dannheiser, only a few years her junior. The *has-senpfeffer* was juicy, even if the service was a little slow. On off hours "Tante," as we called her, was a voracious reader, though she needed a magnifying glass to scan the newspaper. She always had her vices. Tante used to offer toasts like this one to her guests, first in German and then in English: "Alcohol, as you know, is our enemy. But the Bible says, 'You shall also love your enemy.'"

And there was Katharine Hepburn, a role model for independ-ence and survival, in her Fenwick house. Recently, I saw Hepburn's brother-in-law, Ellsworth Grant, who also summers in Fenwick and who himself seems to have dealt reasonably with the aging process. He still writes and peddles the lore of our state to anyone who will listen, or read.

The point is that aging requires us to replace creaky (and worse) body parts with more mind juice, more intent, more purposeful living.

At both sixty and thirty, I lost a spouse to illness. So I am qualified, more than most, to compare the stresses of the two ages. I do know that at sixty I have better friends—friends who gathered around me and who came to the house to clean it and to stuff the freezer with what, judging by the abundant evidence, must be the ultimate meal of grievers: baked lasagna.

I also appreciate much more than ever family ties. From her home in Allentown, Pennsylvania, my daughter, Amy, organized a small gathering to celebrate her father's sixtieth. She gave a brief speech about the turbulent year I'd had and how proud she is of me. I wanted, of course, to turn the tables. And I did so when I told those assembled that in a life of writing and producing and editing, she is my greatest achievement. I know this fact because the process of aging, for all of its difficulties, illuminates the ultimate truths.

The Song Is Me

*I was concerned that this piece would be seen as a bla-
tant example of self-promotion, which of course it was.
So I amused myself by concluding that readers in Connecticut would nonetheless enjoy an inside view of what
it's like to create a musical for the stage. And I was convinced of two things—some of the backstage tales were
worth telling, and the article might help sell tickets (it
did). (Originally published May 2003)*

It is a conversation stopper, this business of writing a musical. People I hadn't seen for a while would ask what I'd been doing. The
usual reply, over the years, was that I'd been working on this or
that. A book, a magazine column. They nodded respectfully. But
when I began working on the lyrics for a musical, well, that made
acquaintances animated and inquisitive. They asked, "What comes
first, the words or the music?" (The answer: neither.) And, "Do
you have a casting couch?" (Details to come.)

Writing a musical is not a frivolous enterprise. A person who
presumes to create such a work tests his capacity to amuse, illumi-
nate, transport, and lift hearts. A lyricist must, in a few brief syllables, move the plot along and provide keen insight to the

character's motives and intentions. The lyrics must create emotion without using loaded words, and they must, of course, suit the melodies of the composer. But I am getting ahead of myself.

I did not get to the historic Ivoryton Playhouse (where Katharine Hepburn, Marlon Brando, Beatrice Lilly, Groucho Marx, and many other luminaries played) overnight. This all began decades ago, the first time I cried over something that happened on the stage, and the first time I left the theater lifted much higher than my modest height, thinking, stupidly, that life is beautiful. It began when I heard touching and inspiring lyrics by Hammerstein, Hart, Loesser, Berlin, Arlen, Sondheim, and W. S. Gilbert. It began with instinct and endured through a career of writing prose—hundreds of thousands of words for articles and books, none of which could be sung.

But along came Steve Metcalf. This was in the early 1980s, when we were both in the newspaper business. Steve made a living as a classical-music critic. But he is also a superb musician himself—a pianist who can play any song in any key and is certainly the life of every party. Cole Porter? Sure. The Beatles or Fats Domino? Sure. He is also a composer. He wrote the music for a show called *Drat!* that had a run off-Broadway. In 1991, the two of us wrote our first song together. Titled "I Love a Sunday Magazine" and modestly amusing, it was tailored to a magazine conference and, therefore, to a limited number of ears. In the years that followed, Steve and I entertained the notion of writing something for a broader audience—a work for the stage that would echo the sentiments of the musicals of old and yet also have something new to say. We needed, of course, a story on which to base it. And that story, or at least the inspiration for it, came out of a basement.

Over a period of two years, I rooted in the archives of the Florence Griswold Museum in Old Lyme, with the idea that the life of Miss Florence, as she was called, was inherently the stuff of compelling theater. Miss Florence had been seen as something of a quaint and independent woman who presided over one of America's most successful artist colonies. A few things had been written about her, but nothing in depth or particularly telling. Many of the American Impressionists she nurtured at that big house went on to successful careers, but she was left behind and died in poverty. To me, this scenario had possibilities. And yet important particulars of Florence's life seemed to be missing. Nothing I could find in those archives suggested a dramatic event on which a stage play could turn. The letters she wrote the artists, and those written to her, were perfunctory. I was ready to give it up until I came across some carefully recorded oral histories of artists in the 1950s who remembered their days at the colony—including vivid recollections of Miss Florence in love with an artist many years younger than she. It appeared that a romantic triangle had ensued. Bingo!

Still, we needed a creative script off of which the songs could be written. And for that Steve and I turned to Colin McEnroe, the writer and radio talk show host who has a great wit and, like us, a longtime affection for musical theater (his father wrote the book for the Broadway musical *Donnybrook*).

We eventually decided against strictly re-creating Florence's life. A period piece would be problematic because it seemed to us to be too limiting. We hoped instead to open up the canvas. We wanted not just painters but artists of other kinds—men and women who sculpt, compose, and write. We lifted the story out of time (a controversial decision among us) in an effort to make it more pertinent to modern lives. We wrote music that embraced a variety of styles, with flavors of classic Broadway, rock 'n' roll, and country. To do all this, we could use Florence's story only as inspiration, not as an end.

The title song came to be written well before there was a script. One of the most persistent supporters of the musical was my wife, Liz, who had come to refer to herself, wryly, as a woman of a certain age. Something about that phrase haunted me.

So, what comes first, the words or the music? Usually, it's the idea. I gave the title, *A Woman of a Certain Age*, to Steve. Two weeks later, he gave me a lilting melody. I took the melody and wrote three verses, a chorus, and an interlude. This was not easy. Song writing is very different from column or book writing, or even poetry. When you think you have it, you don't, because a word that looks appropriate on paper can't easily be sung. I made many changes (some as late as opening night).

We hired a singer to perform the song to a house full of friends. It was an odd feeling, watching people react to words I had written and noting that many of the women in the audience had tears in their eyes. Afterward, several professed astonishment that two men could write a song that affects women in such a way. This affirmation provided an impetus to write more songs when, in fact, we had no guarantee we'd ever get the show produced. The musical theater is competitive. Hundreds of scripts and scores are written every year—most destined for dusty bins.

Liz kept pressing for what she called a grassroots musical movement, the way the hit *Urinetown* started and eventually reached Broadway. We performed in several living rooms with the idea that momentum would build and word would spread. One of the people who helped us along the way, as both a performer of our songs and a networker, was Peter Walker, an experienced Broadway actor. (He was in the original staging of Sondheim's *Follies* and is a lyricist himself—he and Max Showalter wrote *Harrigan & Hart.*) With Peter's assistance we arranged for the trustees of the Ivoryton, and for its executive director, Jacqueline Hubbard, to hear a few songs and a script summary. Jacqui, an accomplished actress who has put on several very successful musicals during her years as Ivoryton's executive director, became an instant fan; she quickly developed ideas about how she would direct the show that would have the same title as its first song.

During auditions, dozens of hopefuls tried to dazzle us with 8-by-10 glossies (resumes pasted on the back) and with their singing and acting abilities. Some had Broadway experience, and some had never been in a professional production. It is a cruel business, the theater. A few performers with enormous talent didn't get a second look—too tall, too old, too young, or too wide for any of our seven roles. But in the end, a cast of first-rate actors and singers was chosen.

No, I had no casting couch—hiring was mostly up to the director, who also didn't have one. This did not stop related talk, however. When Steve and I argued the merits of a fellow who tried out for Frank (the male lead), Jacqui had a different view: not enough sex appeal. She said, "He looks like someone you'd like to mother, not go to bed with."

Even after casting, there were still lyrics to write and rewrite, music to alter, a script to refine, and potential producers from regional theaters and New York City to lure to Ivoryton. Still, this much was already clear: It had been worth every sleepless night when a thousand syllables auditioned in my head.

EPILOGUE

A Woman of a Certain Age made its debut in May 2003, in four workshop performances at the Ivoryton. Steve Metcalf was occupied at one of the two pianos, but Colin McEnroe and I were free to pace in the back of the theater, and to be perplexed whenever the actors altered a line of dialogue or a lyric. Even so, we were elated. Hearing people laugh or sensing their excitement, I thought, "Maybe someday, after all the fixing is done, we can take this to Broadway." I'd love that, of course. But in the spring of 2003, it was quite enough for me to listen to seven professionals sing my words and, at the end of each performance, for the audience to stand and ask the collaborators to take a bow.

The Art of Dying

For her funeral, my wife, Liz, left me a note on a yellow sheet of paper. The things she wanted. Included in that note was the instruction to me not to speak during the service. "Please resist, Lary." When the time came, I of course honored her wish, except to briefly point out to the nearly 400 in attendance that she had offered this instruction, and to read a favorite poem of hers by Billy Collins. She had no instructions, however, about anything I might say after the funeral. And so I felt that, in tribute to her and the way she did what she did, I would take readers into her very private last hours. (Originally published August 2003)

The nurse, whose face was a picture of comfort, asked, "Did anyone give you a tour?" I shook my head, but I would eventually inspect the place on my own—wandering back to things I'd never seen in a hospital, including an enormous living room with a Steinway grand, shelves of books, a six-cornered tank of tropical fish, original art, a kitchen, a suite for overnight guests, a view of a meditation garden. This is part of what Hartford Hospital calls its Palliative Care unit—*palliative*, a gentle name, a name meant to ease, to provide consolation, as death approaches.

My wife, Liz, was just down the hallway in room 406. She was there to recover from a relatively simple procedure the day before to relieve acute symptoms of a terminal case of cancer. Our plan was to go back home to Chester, where she would resume the peaceful process of dying amid her abundant and beautiful azaleas, irises, and lilies. There seemed to be a couple of weeks left, according to Liz and her oncologist, and that's where she preferred to do this.

Early in the day, she had felt reasonably well. She talked about routine matters: What friends we owed dinner to, how to finish a complicated grant for Center City Churches in Hartford, and a feature story that she owed the *Main Street News* in Essex. We also talked about her illness, though we heeded her self-imposed Fifteen-Minute Rule: a quarter of an hour of cancer grousing per day, period.

This fifteen-minute session was packed with a few key points. She had made the right decision a few months earlier. No more treatments. They weren't working anyway, after so many years. She would take charge of her own body, make her own rules, and take full advantage of the time left. She would see her grandchildren, travel, work (just four days earlier she'd spent a half a day at Center City's office), and go out to lunch (the calendar was packed), just as she had always done. She would do this though she had clearly become fatigued, and on occasion short of breath.

Liz was worried about breathing—something akin to drowning, lungs unable to function because of fluid. She was also concerned about how family and friends would remember her; she didn't want the image to be one of an emaciated cancer patient.

At sixty years old, she had tied up the ends of her life. She had made lists about this and that, including what kind of funeral she preferred (though a Christian, Liz asked to have the service at our Chester synagogue). She had dinner with her former husband to talk about their daughters and the grandchildren, and to say good-bye. And she had paid the gardener to not only tend over the summer what she had lovingly built over fifteen years, but to check occasionally to see that the wisteria wouldn't get out of hand and strangle me. Liz had also worked hard on her own spiritual life, advised by the Reverend Dr. Duncan Newcomer of United Church of Chester. The two had talked every week about life and death and about nourishing the soul. Later, Dr. Newcomer would say, "I never met anyone who prepared herself so well, so fully, for what God was preparing for her as Liz Gwillim."

Was I prepared? Not as well—not after twenty years of being with her. Nor was Dianne Bourbeau, Liz's daughter, who was at the hospital during the critical hours and who regularly updated her sister Devon Donahue, in North Carolina, who was frantically trying to arrange with airlines to get to Hartford. And yet I knew what Liz craved: a peaceful and dignified death. All her life she had been a picture of dignity and grace. She also had a beautiful smile.

I wrote a lyric about, in part, that smile. "In the Aftertime of Days," a song about what lasts, was the finale of *A Woman of a Certain Age*. Liz had been the driving force behind that musical, pushing me (the lyricist), Steve Metcalf (the composer), and Colin McEnroe (the script writer). For a while it had seemed as if she wouldn't live to see opening night—an unthinkable scenario. But

Liz rallied—and was, miraculously, a beaming presence in the Ivoryton Playhouse audience. She heard the song inspired by her. An excerpt, from the bridge:

> *Every time I close my eyes I see the smile upon your face,*
> *A smile that lights all time and all space.*
> *What a gift you gave to me as all the years passed swiftly by.*
> *Forgive my silent heart, my faint reply.*

At 3:00 P.M. there was a shift change in the Palliative Care unit—new nurses came onto the floor. The one assigned to our room, Helen, introduced herself to Liz, who was only occasionally conscious by then because we were still giving her a morphine derivative to ease the pain from the procedure.

Helen asked Liz, "Are you comfortable?" Even in her haze Liz knew the right answer. I had taught her the answer over many years—over many attempts to convince her of the wisdom, if not the wit, of the late Henny Youngman. Helen asked again, "Are you comfortable?" Liz replied, "I make a decent living."

Helen smiled, even as I saw tears in her eyes. An hour later, something had changed. Liz's breathing had gotten heavier and more difficult, her skin clammy and cold. Dianne asked Helen if she thought she could go home for the night to Granby. Helen took a moment and said to Dianne, "If I were you, I'd stay." In the language of the Palliative Care unit, this meant that death was imminent.

I have been almost all my life a skeptical Jew. I go to Torah study every Saturday morning at Congregation Beth Shalom Rodfe Zedek in my town and am a member who participates in many ways. But I've had trouble with the concept of God, particularly in regard to human suffering. The feelings are complicated, too much so for a paragraph here. Still, it seemed clear enough that I was beginning to change my thinking—I was beginning to see the natural order of things. For one thing, Helen was taking care of us. Helen, whose name was the same as my late mother's.

Helen wasn't the only angel. There was a whole community of angels in our lives. Hundreds of them. People who supported us. And there was the brilliant and compassionate oncologist, Patricia DeFusco, who tended Liz for nearly twelve years and who considered her to be a challenging patient (questioning everything), one who was fascinated by her disease and wanted to know all there was to know so she could make the right decisions.

After an exhausting day at her Wethersfield treatment center, Pat DeFusco arrived at the hospital at 8:20, just as the final decision had to be made. Liz was breathing heavily, and there was a gurgle in her throat—trouble breathing, just what she (and we) feared. We simply had to give her more morphine, to ease the breathing. But it would also lower her blood pressure. It would, in short, kill her.

Helen administered the final dose. Pat DeFusco went out into the hallway so that Dianne and I could be alone with Liz. Her breathing changed again. Finally, it was becoming much less labored, more natural and painless. But it was becoming very slow. Each breath seemed as if it could be her last. She hadn't moved her arms for several hours, but now Liz moved them—toward me, as if to embrace me. Then she put them back down. And she was gone.

I was consoled by the idea that she had done this in the way she imagined, in the way she insisted—turning a lingering death sentence into something of an ordinary inconvenience, and in the end giving the cancer that killed her very little, if any, gratification. I wanted to shout, "Well done, my dear." And "Brava!" But like Dianne, I simply sat there and squeezed a hand. Pat DeFusco came back into the room and confirmed what we knew.

And then the doctor stood back and said, "Can you believe it? Look at her. She's still beautiful."

About the Author

Lary Bloom has written about the people and lore of Connecticut for twenty-five years, first in the *Hartford Courant* and then as a columnist for *Connecticut* magazine. His books include *The Writer Within*, *When the Game Is on the Line* (coauthored with Rick Horrow), *Alone Together*, *Twain's World* (editor and contributor), and *Something Personal*. Lary also wrote the play *Worth Avenue* and was the lyricist for *A Woman of a Certain Age*. He lives in Chester, Connecticut. For more information, visit www.larybloom.net.